Rent-Seekers, Profits, Wages and Inequality

Péter Mihályi · Iván Szelényi

Rent-Seekers, Profits, Wages and Inequality

The Top 20%

palgrave
macmillan

Péter Mihályi
Department of Macroeconomics
Corvinus University of Budapest
Budapest, Hungary

and

Central European University
Budapest, Hungary

Iván Szelényi
Yale University
New Haven, CT, USA

and

New York University
Abu Dhabi, UAE

ISBN 978-3-030-03845-8 ISBN 978-3-030-03846-5 (eBook)
https://doi.org/10.1007/978-3-030-03846-5

Library of Congress Control Number: 2018961185

This Palgrave Pivot imprint is published by the registered company Springer Nature Switzerland AG
The registered company address is: Gewerbestrasse 11, 6330 Cham, Switzerland

Contents

List of Tables

CHAPTER 1

Introduction

Abstract This book grew out from a partially supportive and partially critical evaluation of Thomas Piketty's best-seller academic monograph, *Capital in the Twenty-First Century*. The authors' main aim is to bring back the concept of rent, developed by David Ricardo two hundred years ago and show that inequalities cannot be explained without the concept of rent and limiting the analysis to profits and wages (as Piketty does) is theoretically false. What matters is not the extent of inequality, but its source. There is nothing generally evil about rents. There are no economies without rent. The two authors, Peter Mihályi, a macroeconomist and Iván Szelényi a sociologist take an interpretative, value-neutral position: some rents are necessary and inevitable, others are destructive.

Keywords Cross-country and within-country inequalities · D. Ricardo's concept of rent · Gini coefficient · Profits and wages

The theme of unjust inequalities has become a central problem of our times. The 2016 US presidential election was fought largely on this issue. The three most important Presidential contenders emphatically criticized the globalized capitalist system precisely for this. In Hillary Clinton's program, out of five propositions, the correction of the

P. Mihályi and I. Szelényi,
Rent-Seekers, Profits, Wages and Inequality,
https://doi.org/10.1007/978-3-030-03846-5_1

wage/profit gap was the third and the fourth most important promise.[1] Donald Trump and Bernie Sanders (for various reasons, Trump for national radicalism, Sanders for social radicalism) went even further. They agreed that, as far as income distribution is concerned, the "entire game is rigged". This intellectual battle has not come to an end with the US elections. In August 2018 *The Economist* newspaper started a one week open debate on its website under the title "Is capitalism rigged in favor of elites?"[2] Out of more than 15 thousand readers who casted their votes, 76% answered "yes".

Arguably, the public political discourse has arrived into a new age. While the question of inequality was a central theme to the nineteenth century economics, in the twentieth century the issues of inequality of distribution of incomes and wealth tended to be neglected in economics (though it emerged as a central theme in sociology). When it was brought back to the center of attention, for instance by Kuznets (1955), it was assumed that economic growth would automatically take care of the issue. Over the past few years, however, the topic has received increasing attention, especially with the path-breaking works of Joseph Stiglitz, *The Price of Inequality* (first published in 2012) and Thomas Piketty's *Capital in the Twenty-First Century* (first published in French in August 2013). Anthony Atkinson (2015) is one of the rare economists who studied income distribution, inequality, and poverty over the past several decades, recently adding another impressive volume *Inequality: What Can Be Done*? to his many publications on the topic. Intriguingly while research of inequality was a way sociologists defined what their profession is, during the past two-three decades most major books were written by economists.

Few scholars share the optimism of Kuznets today: growth is not a guaranteed solution to reduce inequalities. Piketty's main finding and his main prediction were enthusiastically received by many intellectuals, the

[1] "Let's rewrite the rules so more companies share profits with their employees and fewer ship jobs and profits overseas." "Let's make sure that Wall Street, corporations, and the super-rich pay their fair share of taxes." https://www.hillaryclinton.com/feed/five-important-steps-hillary-clinton-will-take-reduce-inequality-and-grow-our-economy/.

[2] To debate this topic, the newspaper invited Jason Furman (Harvard Kennedy School) who argued in favor of the proposition and Deirdre McCloskey (University of Illinois at Chicago) who argued against. https://debates.economist.com/debate/capitalism.

wider public, and several international organizations as *the* right answer to the dilemmas generated by the international financial crisis of 2008.

The question of poverty, always of central concern for sociologists who studied inequality also attracted the attention of economists. The World Bank, which has been the target of criticism of left-leaning sociologist, accusing the institutions for "monetarism" and "neo-liberal economics", "market fundamentalism"[3] took on a leading role in research on poverty. A study of the Bank, beyond offering new careful methods to measure poverty, is also focusing on the future. As it is explained in World Bank (2013), the aim of the ongoing *Shared Prosperity Program* is to condense extreme poverty from the present 20% below 3% by 2030 at the world level through policies targeting the bottom 40% of the income scale in each and every country of the world. Concurrently, in a flagship publication of the OECD (2015) experts claimed that income inequality had had a sizeable and statistically significant negative impact on the long-term growth in 19 core OECD countries between 1990 and 2010. In an IMF staff-paper—Ostry et al. (2014)—similar findings were reported. Note, however, that these econometric works are challenged by others. E.g. Fuest et al. (2018) compiled a data set covering 110 countries over the years from 1970 to 2010 and run multivariate regressions pertaining to the growth—inequality linkage with control variables depicting the sample countries' other political and social characteristics. Their conclusion, not very surprising for the present authors, was that a negative correlation between inequality and growth can only be detected if per capita GDP remains below 5000 US dollars.

When economists or sociologists start writing about inequalities, it is indispensable to start with numerous caveats. First, and foremost, wealth concentration is twice the level of income inequality across the advanced market economy countries.[4] Secondly, everywhere in the world, political discussions on inequality often conflate two related but distinct issues: equality of income and wealth on the one hand, and equality of opportunities and social mobility on the other. As the title of our book promises,

[3]Joseph Stiglitz who was chief economist of the World Bank for a while shared this view, so his tenure was cut short. As he left he received very negative reviews (see for instance the rather vitriolic "The bumpy ride of Joe Stiglitz," *The Economist*, December 16, 1999), though in the past 15 years the Bank came closer to Stiglitz's vision.

[4]See the recent OECD publication covering 28 member countries by Balestra and Tonkin (2018).

three sources of income inequalities—wages, profits, and rents—are in the focus of our research. The long-term social consequences of wealth inequalities—for instance on fluidity, or relative mobility—are mentioned in the book several times, but we don't claim to say anything particularly novel on this.[5]

All specialists of the subject know that there are intrinsic difficulties in measuring the levels of statistical inequality in a precise way. In medium-size and small countries, survey methods are simply not suitable to obtain reliable information of the top 1% or the top 0.1% of the population. Even incomes of the top 10% are difficult to estimate due to the increasing refusal rate in surveys. The smaller is the country, the bigger is the measurement error arising from this. If the measurement of absolute levels is difficult, it is also difficult to assess the changes in inequality in the short-run, say during the 3–4 years of tenure of a given government. It is very common that the two most widely used indicators move into opposite directions in such a short time (i.e. the Gini coefficient and the percentage share of people living at a pre-defined poverty level). Although conceptually it is easy to make a distinction between pre-tax and after-tax incomes, in real life, it is difficult to know whether the system of taxation is not sufficiently progressive[6] or the crux of the problem is merely tax evasion (cheating). A further statistical complication arises from the fact that the Gini coefficient is not applicable to measure wealth inequalities, if many households report negative wealth—which is actually quite common among young families living in their own houses burdened with a long-term mortgage.

Our last caveat pertains to the seemingly paradoxical impact of globalization. Rapidly increasing foreign trade and various forms of foreign direct investments lead to the **cross-country** equalization of incomes (e.g. if China and the United States are compared), while the **within-country** inequalities rise both in the most advanced economies (such as the United States), and in the emerging countries (like China or India), as well as in the post-communist countries (like Poland). And this is true for other types of geographic aggregations, like Europe

[5]Instead, we wholeheartedly recommend Robert D. Putnam's (2015) masterful account of the visible erosion of social mobility which occurred during the lifetime of two American generations.

[6]Few supporters of the progressive income tax system know that this idea was first coined by Marx and Engels in *The Communist Manifesto* (1848).

or the European Union. As it was pointed out by Darvas (2016) and others, when low-income countries in a given region grow faster than high-income countries, **global inequality**—i.e. the inequality among individuals living on Earth, on the European continent or in the European Union—is decreasing even if national (within-country) inequalities are growing.

This latter point is not merely a statistical fact. The two types of inequality changes pointing into the opposite direction are causally related. If we stay with the China–US comparison, it is trivial that the rapid rise of the Chinese workers' wages is a consequence of the world-wide expansion of Chinese manufacturing industry, and this exerts a downward pressure on the wages of low-skilled US workers who are more and more forced to compete internationally with their Chinese counterparts. Branko Milanovic (2016) findings are consistent with our assertion. Cross-country income inequality (measured by Gini) increased steadily if we do not weight countries by the size of their population. However, if we weight for population, there is a dramatic decline of global income inequality since 1980 and this can be attributed especially to the rise of China (to some extent the rise of India), the increasing inequalities in wealthy countries and the extreme poverty of many very small countries, especially in Africa.

1 Back to David Ricardo

The main purpose of this book—the sixth within a series of writings on this subject[7]—is to "bring rents back in", a concept largely neglected by mainstream economics and sociology. In a way, we turn from John Locke (1632–1704), Adam Smith (1723–1790) and Karl Marx (1818–1883) to David Ricardo (1772–1823) in search of a theoretically sound explanation of inequalities.

Our initial inspiration to think about the issue came from Thomas Piketty's above-mentioned book. In Piketty's concept, the absolute size of the gap between r and g (where r is the annual net rate of return in percentage form on the assets owned by capitalists and g is the economy's annual growth rate) explains the statistically observable magnitude of and variations in wealth inequality. His innovation is the $r > g$

[7] See Mihályi and Szelényi (2016a, b, c, d, 2017).

formula. If $r > g$ holds that leads necessarily and immediately to growing inequalities.

Unlike in the Marxian model, here in Piketty's two-class model, the relationship between g and r is not fixed in time or in space, theoretically all possibilities are permitted ($r = g$, $r>g$, $r < g$). But historically, on the basis of his own statistical estimations covering the period from the Antiquity until 2012, Piketty claims that in the world as a whole, and more certainly in Britain and France, r was significantly larger than g (4–5% vs. 1–2%) most of the time, except for the last hundred years. His model is a zero-sum dynamic game because it is assumed that the wage and salary earners do not have (net) savings ($s_w = 0$), therefore they cannot accumulate private wealth (W). By contrast, the upper classes, especially the top of the upper class, the top 1 or 0.1% of the families are modeled with exceptionally high savings from profits ($s_\Pi \approx 1$) and cost-effective financial investment strategies thanks to the diminishing relative wealth-management costs. Thus, these elites appropriate a higher and higher proportion of national income at the expense of everyone else.

With the $r > g$ formula Piketty offered a simple definition what in his view the overarching social problem of the twenty-first century will be. The accumulation of incomes and wealth in the top 1 or top 0.1% is increasing and this leads to slower economic growth or may even lead to stagnation. Those at lower ranks in society have less and less of a chance to climb to the top. The top is increasingly reproducing itself like a new aristocracy. As a result, liberal capitalism tends to become "**patrimonial capitalism**"; the class order of liberal capitalism becomes rigid rank order. This is a powerful intellectual statement and a promising program for the "we are the 99 percent" movement.

In this book, we diverge from Piketty's account in two important respects. We are deeply skeptical about his central explanation, namely that in advanced market economies excessive growth of profits is the fundamental reason for inequalities, which, in turn, slow down growth and generate popular dissatisfaction in the long run.

First, we are not persuaded by his definition of r. Piketty defines r as "return on capital". If we take for granted that competition is not perfect on many vitally important markets, one needs to make a critical distinction between "profit" and "rent". It leads to wrong conclusions to mingle all types of non-wage income as profits.

Let us start from the classical theory's equation under perfect competition:

$$\text{National Income} = \text{Profits}\,(\Pi) + \text{Wages}\,(W) + \text{Rents}\,(R),$$

or in growth form, when subsequent years are compared:

$$\Delta\,\text{National Income}\,(g) = \Delta\Pi + \Delta W + \Delta R$$

In classical theory, profit (Π) is defined as the value of the total annual return on capital, wages (W) as the price of labor for a year, rent as the annual payment to the owners of land (agricultural land and in addition, control over the location of production, on possession of natural resources). Locke, Smith, Ricardo, and Marx would all agree in such a statement. Whether rents contribute to g is disputable (classical theorists do have some doubts or are explicit that it does not).

Hence for us, $r > g$ is a sensible proposition as long as r is defined as "rent" and not as profits *à la* Piketty. In advanced economies, the long-run average of g is about 1.5–2.0% annually, thus a higher r (above 2%) can sound credible as a starting assumption. But if we assume for profits and wages perfect competition, this is a BIG assumption. We know that there is no empirically observable market where competition is perfect. Nevertheless, short of any better heuristic device, we start with this assumption our book. Then we will explore systematic deviations from perfect competition for both and wages. We will show for capital (monopolies, oligopolies, and cartels) and labor (trade unions, strong labor/social democratic governments, and large welfare states) that they do deviate from those magnitudes, which would be earned on markets under the conditions of perfect competition. The bottom line of our argument is that in competitive markets—though not necessarily *perfectly* competitive (!)—higher profits and higher wages tend to contribute to higher growth and greater wealth for all.

As far as rent is concerned—following Ricardo's theory—our assumption is that r does not contribute to growth. Rent is a symptom of wealth, not its source. In a way, rent is excess income, but it does not follow through that rent is always undeserved or rent is "evil" in some sense. We will show in this book that some forms of rent may even be necessary (and useful) for social stability and market innovation. Therefore, when Piketty defines rents as all kinds of non-wage income, he makes an error[8]; an ahistorical generalization about the "general laws"

[8] In Mihályi and Szelényi (2016b) we showed that the historical underpinning of Piketty's own $r > g$ model was a statistical artifact, arising from the intermingling of the concept of profit and rent on the one hand, and private capital (K) and wealth on the other.

of capitalism (something we will argue in this book does not exist and comes close to the conclusion that he actually never makes) that the collapse of capitalism is inevitable.

Let us make just a brief note about history. Rent in our view is the dominant—or occasionally even exclusive—source of income and wealth in pre-capitalist economies. Only capitalist economies are driven by profit and wage maximizing behavior. The strong point of Piketty's is that rent-seeking may be playing an increasing role nowadays. But we are inclined to interpret this more "re-feudalization" (his use of the term "patrimonial capitalism" is consistent with this assumption) rather than a return to "classical" capitalism of pre-twentieth century, especially to the pre-1930 epoch as Piketty seems to imply. In this book, we follow the "varieties of capitalisms" paradigm. Piketty seems to assume that pre-twentieth century capitalism was ruled by the "general laws" of capitalism, without being particularly specific about what they are. According to him, the epoch between 1930 and 1970 was a deviation from this "general laws" and now capitalism is returning to its "normal" stage.

In contrast with Piketty's argument, our general hypothesis is, that higher profits and wages most of the time add to g—the annual growth of national income (or GDP). Rents on the other hand usually reduce g. Some moderation of g (hence some r) may be useful and necessary, but if r is "excessive" (or to be more precise, if profit and wage maximizing behavior is replaced or at least overweight by rent-seeking behavior), that is likely to lead to economic stagnation, or even decay and social conflicts.

In pre-capitalist societies where rent was the dominant form of income g was very low—a fraction of 1%. With the dawn of the twentieth century, we have probably entered into a new phase of capitalism, "patrimonial capitalism"; where g is lower than it was in the twentieth century and where again rent can be an increasingly important source of social prestige and privilege. We regard this observation of Piketty as the most intriguing and persuasive one. But unlike Piketty we do not regard this as the return to the "general laws" of capitalism (neither do we see the "social democratic" dramatic reduction of inequalities in Northern Europe and the United States during the post-World War II years as a "deviation" from the normal model—which in our view does not exist), but as **a new phase of "generic" capitalism**.

Second, we would like to make a contribution to the inquiries on inequality by focusing on the upper middle class. Piketty—like most of the popular reflection of the increased inequalities during the past 40 years—tend to focus on the increased income/wealth gap between the top 1 or 0.1% and the rest of the society.[9] There are indeed dramatic data on how much wealth of the world owned by the top 1.0 or 0.1%, what the income gap is now between ordinary workers and CEO's. This all needs attention, but the question we keep asking in this book: to what extent this explains the transition to "patrimonial capitalism".

If a society becomes patrimonial, it implies that it becomes "hereditary", the next generation inherits the privileges of the previous one. As far as we can tell this is not particularly likely on the very top. Unfortunately, we do not have comprehensive data on this. But indirect evidences are abundant. There are many people who climbed up to the very top from very low positions—due to good luck or special talent. If you look at the net worth of the wealthiest Americans in the *Forbes* 2018 list, you can find many who come from middle class background. Bill Gates's ($90 billion) father was a prominent lawyer, but in no way in the top 1%. The same goes for Mark Zuckenberg ($71 billion), the son of a dentist and even more so for Larry Ellison ($59 billion), who was an adopted child and grew up in a middle class neighborhood. George Soros, a Hungarian immigrant arrived to the US penniless and became a multi-billionaire.[10] In post-communist countries of Central Europe, Russia, and China, the new rich are coming typically from rather humble origins. Hence, many at the top do not reproduce themselves; they climb up from the upper middle class or even the middle class. This is probably even more so for the top 1% of incomes. Extraordinary income earners in sports, arts, science come from even more diverse backgrounds. Extraordinary incomes (and wealth) on the very top may come from market competition and is not particularly "patrimonial" in character. Paradoxically, this applies to a certain extent to some of the princes of Saudi Arabia and other billionaires close to the throne. They are super-rich today, but their parents or grandparents were not.

[9] Oxfam, the renowned charity timed the publication of its fresh research for the opening of the Davos economic summit and skillfully captured the headlines of many newspapers. Another sensational formulation of the same report was that "85 richest people on the planet have the same wealth as the poorest 50% (3.5 billion people)" Jacobs (2015).

[10] In 2017, Soros's net worth was estimated at $25 billion, but in early 2018, Soros had a net worth of merely $8 billion, after donating $18 billion to his philanthropic agency, the Open Society Foundations.

When it comes to the upper middle class (somewhere in the top 10–20%), the story is quite different. These are rather closed social positions, it is difficult to climb into or fall out from it. The most provocative hypothesis of the present book is as follows: the socially and economically crucial difference is NOT between the 1 and 99%, but it is more likely to be the top 10–20% and with the rest of 80–90% is the circumstance that Russian President Putin's illiberal democracy model[11] survived apparently free—though arguably not fair—elections can be explained by the fact that autocratic leaders often have a large population of clients, who economically benefit from the illiberal system. At the same time, a great deal of the illiberal politicians' support comes from the not well-off population who vote for them because they share the traditionalist ideology advocated by the illiberal leaders (patria, religion, heterosexual marriage, being afraid of strangers, the other "others", etc.).

As we have already recalled, the received wisdom since Adam Smith was that income has to be distributed to the three "factors" of production (capital, labor, and land) as profits, wages, and rent. The critical question to evaluate "inequality" was whether such a distribution was "fair" or not. But it was assumed that all owners of each of those factors are entitled to an income, a share of the newly created wealth. While Smith had ambiguous views about the "fair" share of rent—at a number of occasions in *The Wealth of Nations* he expressed some doubts how much rent-collectors contributed to the creation of wealth (or new value)—but he assumed that at least some if not all of the rent was "earned income". On the other hand, Ricardo saw rent as a symptom and not as a source of wealth. This was an insight Marx did not

[11]This term is usually attributed to F. Zakaria (1997) who used it to describe electoral regimes in developing countries, where leaders who exercised authoritarian rule nevertheless won popular elections. Viktor Orbán, the Hungarian prime minister in a speech on July 16, 2014 called the system he tries to implement in Hungary as illiberal democracy, digging this concept hidden for some twenty years in the ivory towers of political science and turning it into an integral part of political discourse. Whether his project is democratic has been hotly debated, but the term illiberal was not only widely accepted, and was now used to describe not only Hungary during the Orbán regime but also countries like Putin's Russia or Erdogan's Turkey. Orbán criticized liberalism as ignoring national interest. Csillag and Szelényi (2015) interpreted this as a project, which aims to maximize the power of the executive branch of the government (as the only agency which can see beyond individual interest and represent the "common good") at the expenses of the autonomy of legislature and judiciary.

appreciate and created a theory of exploitation, in which profits as much as rents were unearned incomes, the only source of new values was labor. Chapter 2 of this book reviews the history of idea of "rent" in classical socio-economic theory.

Over the past 40 or so years, Ricardo's theory had a come-back. Since the late 1960s economist (Tullock 1967; Krueger 1974; Congleton et al. 2008) identified rent-seeking behavior as economically unproductive. A few sociologists advocated a rent based theory of class and exploitation. Our book was inspired by the work of the Danish-born American inequality theorist, Aage Sorensen (1941–2001), but rather than going all the way to develop a theory of class and exploitation we shall use Max Weber's work on rent and we make both a historical and analytic distinction between rents and profits. As we shall argue later, the notion of exploitation cannot be operationalized without building it on the labor theory of value, a concept we entirely reject. Weber's distinction between "closed" and "open" social relations offers us a better tool to locate the rent/profit distinction both historically and analytically and give a sociological content to it.

Our preferred income concept in this book is net (after-tax) household income, equivalized to take differences in household size/composition into account. The income-sharing unit is the household, while the unit of analysis is the individual member of the household. This is how the Gini coefficient is calculated most of the time. As we already noted, the size and the nature of inequalities in income and wealth are not identical (private wealth is more unequally distributed than after-tax wages), but the trends of the two phenomena are similar both across countries and within a given country in time. This is almost self-evident since wealth is essentially the result of accumulated incomes. It also accepted in the scholarly literature—including the most recent pieces of research—that the income/wealth inequalities are reflected in many other welfare indicators, such as health status,[12] consumption, education, and mortality.[13] However, all these consequences are beyond the scope of our book.

As a non-controversial, convenient starting point of this introductory chapter, we shall use the scale of a recently published ILO-EU study

[12]Deaton (2013).

[13]Attanasio and Pistaferri (2016). For a Good Collection of Papers on Inequality Beyond Income, see the Special Issue of the *Journal of Economic Perspective*, Vol. 30. No. 2. Spring 2016.

Table 1 The relative size of income classes based on net household income, in percentage (25 selected EU countries, 2011)

ILO classification	*Percentage of median income*	*Lowest (%)*	*Highest (%)*
Top	Above 200	Sweden: 3	Latvia: 14
Upper middle class	120–200	Portugal: 25	Luxembourg: 30
Core middle class	80–120	Latvia: 23	Denmark: 40
Lower middle class	60–80	Denmark: 12	Luxembourg: 19
Bottom	Up to 60	Czech Republic: 13	Lithuania: 25

Source ILO's own calculations based on the EU-SILC database, downloaded from http://www.ilo.org/wcmsp5/groups/public/—dgreports/—dcomm/documents/publication/wcms_535617.pdf

(2016) in the form of a five-group classification of the entire income distribution.

The relative size of the top and bottom income strata varies significantly among the countries of Europe. For example, in Sweden, only 3% of households belong to the rich and this is the lowest figure among the EU countries in the sample. By contrast, Latvia represents the other extreme, where 14% of households command per capita incomes more than two times bigger than the national average. The detailed data also show a more substantial middle class in the Nordic countries—Denmark and Sweden—and a smaller middle class in both the south (Greece and Spain) and in Central and Eastern Europe (Estonia, Latvia, and Lithuania). If we had similar data for non-European countries they would probably show a much bigger variation. As we noted already, we believe in the "variety of capitalism" concept.

Of course, we are fully aware of the inherent measurement problems, even beyond those we already mentioned on the very first pages of this chapter. These are important and it is safe to say that all surveys—including the one we used in Table 1—are underestimating inequalities to a certain extent. There are numerous reasons for this. There is a disconnecting between macroeconomics and the statistical evidence used in the studies on economic inequality. Macroeconomics relies on national accounts data to study the growth of GDP/GNP, while inequality studies rely on individual or household income, survey, and tax data. Ideally, all three sets of data should be consistent, but they are not. The total flow of income reported by households in survey or tax data adds up to barely 60% of the incomes recorded in the national accounts, with this gap increasing over the past several decades.[14] However, we will not try to correct the data produced by others and pretend that "we know better".

If we look back into the past, the second half of the twentieth century, rather than at the present, the following stylized facts can be derived from the literature.

1. In the decade *prior* to 1990, the lowest value of Gini coefficient in the world was found in the former socialist countries of Eastern Europe. Typically, it was well below 0.25, while in the majority of OECD economies its value was only slightly below or around 0.25 (e.g. Japan, West Germany, Belgium, The Netherlands, Italy, Sweden, and Finland). In certain English-speaking liberal countries (e.g. Canada, UK, Australia), Gini was in the range of 0.25–0.30, while in the United States it fluctuated in the 0.32–0.36 range.[15] In the advanced OECD countries, the intertemporal variance of "within-country" inequality was smaller than the cross-country variance of within-country inequalities. In other words, countries could live quite well with different levels of inequalities for quite a while.[16]
2. Today, two groups can be formed from the East European post-communist countries. In the first group, the inequality change *after* 1990 was less than 0.10 points (e.g. Czech Republic, East Germany, Poland, and Slovakia). In the second group, change was equal or bigger than 0.10 points (e.g. Bulgaria, Estonia, Hungary, Latvia, Lithuania, and Romania).[17]
3. Since 1990, within-country inequalities have been increasing in three major regions of the world: the USA, the EU15, and the post-communist countries. If countries forming the EU28 group are considered as a single region (i.e. after the accession of some of the former European communist states), inequality has

[14] Many important forms of income, such as fringe benefits of employees, retained profits and taxes paid by corporations, or imputed rent of homeowners, are part of GNP, but are not included in individual survey or tax data (Piketty et al. 2016).

[15] Tóth (2014).

[16] Ibid.

[17] Ibid.

been declining within EU28 as well—due to the catching up the post-communist countries in per capita income.[18]

4. As we shall explain later, within-country inequalities often have historical roots in the pre-capitalist past. Ethno-racial, religious discriminations, sectarian, clan, and regional conflicts are still the major drivers of the systematic stratification of inequalities in many parts of the world. The good news is that in spite of the disquieting level of such inequalities, in many countries the gap between the privileged and the underprivileged ethnic, religious, etc., groups has been narrowing already for several decades.

* * *

After presenting the full social picture in Table 1, we are now narrowing our focus further. From here onwards, we are concentrating our attention only on the upper part of the inequalities. *Why are the rich, the top 10–20% of the people, rich*—this is our research question. In a short sentence, our answer is that rents—rather than profits as conventionally held—are the real culprits.

In Ricardo's opinion, R vs. $(\Pi + W)$ was a negative-sum game under the historical conditions he was familiar with. This is a meaningful proposition even today. The relative weight of R as compared to $\Pi + W$ still matters in quantitative sense, and it also matters qualitatively, how R is achieved; whether this is conceived as fair and legitimate in the eyes of the voters.

Let's begin with the legitimacy issue. Rent-seeking can be seen and is often seen as **corruption**. Whether a practice is corrupt or not is a matter of social judicial judgment. But even in the most legal rational authority many economic practices which do not meet the moral approval of society cannot always be regulated by law. We may call an act corrupt, which in a smart way by-passes the laws, but nevertheless purposefully limits competition to office holders and or their client's benefits. There are many examples of this in the pharmaceutical industry, in military procurements and of course in post-communist societies, in privatization. There are also ample examples of corruption in honorable institutions, such as wage negotiations or helping the poor. Trade unions may make behind the doors deal with employers at the expense of laid-off

[18] Darvas (2016).

colleagues; social workers often exclude the poorest of the poor from benefits based on ethno-racial or gendered prejudices. Such practices may not break the laws, but on ethical ground can be judged corrupt.

2 Inequalities and Social Stability

Before we move further, let us put the institution of rent in brackets for a moment, as if it did not exist or did not matter for the society. As long as wages are on the rise, this is a positive-sum game, as we argued above. Neoclassical equilibrium models are all based on this assumption, which was perhaps not very far from reality until recently. Globalization, however, has brutally changed the outcome of the game.[19] While profits have been rising in many sectors of the USA, Germany, and other big economies, real wages in the same sectors stagnated for many years as a consequence of—*inter alia*—outsourcing and the growing share of the financial sector. Hence, we agree with Piketty that today the wage–profit relationship in the advanced Western countries could become a negative-sum game for low-skilled workers and employees, which in turn fuels populist sentiments against globalization, migration, and the highly educated, highly paid business executives.

Having said this, we still assert that inequality is only loosely related to economic growth or social stability. In some societies—in the United States for instance—high inequalities are accepted and the United States produces relatively fast growth and social stability with Gini even over 0.40. Some other societies (in Scandinavia for instance) people do not tolerate inequality well, but they can still produce good growth rates and great social stability. In most cases, contrary to Piketty's two-class model logic, persistent (real) wage growth counts more in the eyes of voters than a shift in the wage/profit relationship at the detriment of wages.

The current that can be seen as running counter to Piketty is that increasing levels of inequality do not necessarily lead to political instability. Important counter-examples can be observed both in Western and post-communist democracies and post-communist authoritarian regimes. The underprivileged poor are inclined to abstain from voting in elections. This holds for such divergent countries as the United States or Hungary, and the political elites are fully aware of this. In a

[19] See Solow (2015) which bluntly acknowledges this.

vote-maximizing strategy, pro-poor policies simply do not pay off. In authoritarian China, where elections are largely ceremonial, inequalities skyrocketed, but so far, the popular response was mute. Since 1978 economic growth was phenomenal, the boats of hundreds of millions were lifted out of poverty with the rising tides, even though at very unequal speed.[20] People, therefore, may have accepted more inequalities as long as their prospects for a better life seemed secure. Martin Whyte (2010) found that inequality was not a major concern for the ordinary Chinese. Russia had similar experiences during the first few years of the twenty-first century.[21]

We do not advocate "uprooting" the capitalist system, to abolish private property and the monopolistic position it means—at any moment of time—for the owners of capital for the sake of greater meritocracy, more efficiency in the use of the national wealth—like, for example, Posner and Weyl (2018) do in their startlingly popular, new book. In the last chapter of the present book, we propose a more comprehensive use of the inheritance tax, but we don't want to use this or similar wealth taxes to force *everyone* in the society to drastically reduce the volume of assets he or she owns with the threat of taxing their wealth away from them. (We have to confess, that the main idea of the Posner and Weyl book, the concept of *social dividend*, strongly resembles us to the utopian proposal of a hardly known, Hungarian economist, Tibor Liska (1925–1994). In the Liska-model, property was fully open to competition as gaining control over property in regular, public auctions was regarded as a fundamental human right. The model allowed the state to have only regulatory functions, but zero ownership and zero redistribution of incomes. The Liska-model had been widely discussed in the Hungarian reform debates in the 1980s, but in the end, it was not seriously considered as a real alternative to Western-type market systems.[22])

[20] In Chapter 6 we shall demonstrate this mechanism with a simple arithmetic example.

[21] The Mihályi and Szelényi (2017) paper is entirely devoted to the role of rents in the transition process from the pre-1989 socialist to the present day capitalist system.

[22] Nevertheless, the Liska-model was not entirely unknown in its own time to the Western public. Norman Macrae (1983), the legendary Deputy Chief Editor of the *The Economist* magazine wrote a long and enthusiastic paper in his newspaper. For a more recent, English-language write up of the Liska-model, see http://www.liska.hu/fliska/seconomy.htm.

Furthermore, everyday experience, as well as academic research shows that ordinary people have little idea about the true (i.e. statistically measured) size of inequalities in their own countries. Gimpelson and Treisman (2015) demonstrated on a variety of large, cross-national surveys that what people think they know is often wrong. In their list of 40 countries, the "least correctly informed" people are the citizens of 8 post-communist countries (Ukraine, Hungary, Croatia, Slovak Republic, Estonia, Poland, Slovenia, and the Czech Republic); while on the top of the list we find two rich welfare states (Norway and Denmark).[23] Moreover, they showed that the *perceived level of inequality*—and not the actual level—strongly correlates with the ideologically motivated demand for redistribution and the reported conflicts between the rich and the poor.

What really annoys people—ordinary people and social scientists alike—is the knowledge *or* the presumption that successful entrepreneurs and especially the most successful ones are greedy, dishonest and corrupt. In the North American media, during the recent financial crisis, "Main Street" represented the interests of everyday people and small business owners, in contrast with "Wall Street" (in the United States) or "Bay Street" (in Canada), symbolizing the interests of highly paid managers working for large banks and corporations. In Southern European countries, like Bulgaria, Romania or Greece or in Latin America, where corruption is especially common, this interpretation of the last 10 years since 2008 can be seen as the leading explanation for political instability and the strikingly low trust in market institutions as such.

As we will show in the next chapter on the example of Ricardo's failure to predict "scientifically" the rise of scarcity rent for agricultural land, it is inherently impossible to predict the future trends of other types of scarcity rents, too. The last 20 years exemplified that rents on oil and gas extraction can vary enormously and with this the relative income position of the workers as well. The same explanation holds for the case of Norway and the UK, if compared to France of Italy. In Central and Eastern Europe, the "free" money flowing from the European Union

[23]The list was compiled from a questionnaire, where people were asked to choose the income distribution diagram with the Gini coefficient closest to the correct one for their country in 2009. On the top, 61% of the Norwegian respondents made the right choice concerning the distribution of post-tax-and-transfer incomes, while in Ukraine only 5 (!) percent of the respondents were right.

has been the chief motivation of rent-seeking practices of those firms, individuals, local governments, etc., which feel themselves close to the center of political power, where the access to EU funds is controlled.

So what is to be done? We return here again to Ricardo. He suggested that the best system of taxation is a tax on rent. Tax on income (be it from wages or profit) tends to have inflationary affect, tax on rent does not. "Tax the 1 percent" is populist demagoguery anyway. There is no way how one can generate enough public income just taxing the wealthiest 1%. The fairest tax system is on inheritance. True enough, there are practical limits how much tax can be charged to rent (and especially to inheritance), some progressive income tax on wages and profits is inevitable, but the policy this book supports shifts taxation from incomes to taxation to rent.

3 Gist of the Book

The structure of the remaining part of the book is as follows. In this chapter, we offer a review of classical economic theories from Locke to Smith, Ricardo, and Marx and later a review of political and sociological theory. The starting point is John Locke, the founder of the modern version of the labor theory of value. While he emphasized that all value is being created by labor, he concedes that as soon as capital is accumulated and land ownership becomes private, owners of capital and land will also contribute to the creation of value. The second half of this chapter tries to locate the question of rent/profit, open/close relations in historical context. Most of the literature on rent (especially the one on rent-seeking) sees rent as a destructive force, often similar or identical with corruption. In pre-capitalist formations incomes typically came from rent. Rent collection was usually justified by tradition and was rarely seen as corruption.

We take an "interpretative", somewhat value-neutral position (we see some rents as economically socially necessary, others destructive). There is nothing generally evil about rent. We know no economies without rent. Even in advanced societies, rent complements profits, often in order to create social stability. Medicaid, unemployment benefit, etc., recipients also collect "rent" (income they did not earn).

Furthermore, to protect incentives for innovation, innovators, exceptionally creative people, may also receive rents, to protect them against ongoing—and potentially destructive—competition on the market. But beyond a certain level (what that is may remain to be elaborated) rent-seeking in modern societies leads to state failure and/or economic–social crisis.

Indeed, some of rent-seeking can become economically (and socially) destructive. The classical case of economically destructive rent-seeking under liberal capitalism is **market capture by corporations**. Large corporations or groups of corporations can establish monopolies, oligopolies or cartels and sell products or services over market prices, hence collect rent. **State capture by oligarchs** (extremely wealthy individuals capturing state positions to promote their individual wealth) does also happen—though less typically—under market capitalism. "Robber barons" in the nineteenth century United States—to a large extent—"captured the state"—bribed public officials to pass legislation, which served their interest. Democrats (and some Republicans) in the United States assert that this is the essence of the new Trump administration. Trump resists putting his business dealing in trusts, using his presidential power to endorse the business interest of his children/family, appointing secretaries to the administration with deep business interest.

Rent destruction can even be the source of social instability. The best example is the impact of globalization in the core countries in the world system. Some social strata—including sections of the working class—were protected from competition from peripheral countries for centuries. Globalization threatened some of such privileged—and their rents. This helps to explain the anti-globalization, anti-migration populist appeal from the political left and right, especially to the white working class (and for some of the white upper middle class). During the 2016 US elections, Sander and Trump appealed to the dissatisfaction of white working class with globalization, the same political consideration led to Brexit the same year in Great Britain.

Chapter 3 offers an analysis of 13 types of rents derived from two main categories of rents: **scarcity rents** and **solidarity rents**. We strongly believe that only such differentiated categorization can adequately explain the different forms of rent-seeking and—through this—elucidate why many forms of rents are functioning as intrinsic building blocks of enlightened, liberal market economies. In short: rents and rent-seeking cannot be eliminated from our system. In Chapter 4, we analyze the class reproduction of the upper middle class. Our central hypothesis is that the most consequential change in the system of social inequalities is not the increasing share of incomes and wealth by the top 1 or 0.1%, but the shrinking relative mobility into and from the top 10–20%. There is a trend for those on the top of social hierarchy to become a sort of "new nobility", a "dominant rank or estate" where people are born into. We identify three mechanisms of such a class reproduction: elite education, inheritance of wealth and assortative mating. In this upper middle class—we hypothesize—increasing proportion of incomes and wealth can be interpreted as rent. Given inherited privileges people in this class or estate, some and increasing proportion of their income and wealth in "unearned", a critical proportion of their wealth is inherited, part of their higher income is rewarding credentials, prestigious degrees from elite universities rather than just return on their human capital investments.

In Chapter 5 we turn our attention to the most recent stages of post-communist transformation. Our aim is to show that rent-seeking works in many important dimensions differently from the practices of the advanced liberal democracies, although the basic mechanisms of rent-seeking under market conditions exist as well. In the process of making markets and especially in fast privatization during post-communist transition, political elites inevitable intervened into the market processes (they "created markets"—to put it with Polanyi). In such instances, political bosses manipulate the markets. The propertied bourgeoisie has to be created, so those in political office have to allocate property to those whom they trust. When this happens, some may also use their political office to enrich themselves or their families beyond the socially accepted norms. This can continue even after market institutions were created. Allocation of EU grants in several new member states is a typical case. The question is: to what extent the privileged clients are "*Strohmann*"-s of political elites. Some call this the "mafia state"; hence a state where the goal-function of the government is the enrichment of the political elite. In this regard, we are somewhat skeptical, we tend to believe that the main goal of such governments is to obtain and maintain power and especially as long as they operate in an electoral democracy they need clients to win elections. But the main point is: we just do not have the data, thus we cannot prove our conjectures.

Once a new propertied bourgeoisie has been created they occasionally might have political ambitions (this certainly was the case in later years of Yeltsin's rule). A post-communist form of "state capture by oligarchs" did indeed exist, though political elites tend to be on the counter-attack, which might lead to an **oligarch capture by political elites**. This was the great innovation of Putin already in 2000. Putin put the new rich to loyalty test, those who failed and were unwilling to abandon political ambitions were either exiled or put in jail and their property was allocated to loyal clients.

Chapter 6 deals with the rent securing function of nation states and rent destruction capacities of globalization. Globalization is often seen as a tyranny of multi-nationals (and their rent-seeking). We do not deny this. To the extent, multi-nationals achieve monopoly they may be rent-collectors, but usually, multi-nationals have to compete with other multi-nationals, hence they adopt profit-seeking behaviors. In contrast, nation-states—in particular at the core of the world system—tend to defend their nationals (workers, businessmen, and intellectuals) from competition of the non-nationals. With the 2015 refugee crisis and Donald Trump's campaign, **migration** became the most critical issue, and it did steal the attention from the issues of increasing inequalities within nation states.

Finally, Chapter 7 briefly summarizes the theoretical and policy conclusions. The main theoretical ambition of the book is the change the discourse about inequality. There are two important policy conclusions:

- What matters is not the extent of inequality, but its source. The Gini coefficient of inequality can range between 0.2 and 0.4 and produce equally stable and dynamic society as long as allocation is meritocratic, as long as inequality is between wages and profits under perfect competition. Inequality becomes a major social (and economic issue) if it is driven by rent. Rent driven inequality undermines the meritocratic legitimacy of liberal capitalism and the efficiency of capital investments.
- Discourse about inequality focused during the past few years on the top 1.0, or top 0.1%. This in our view is misleading. On the very top of the income pyramid, social mobility tends to be high and it is less of a political concern. But there is not only a growing gap between the top 10–20% versus the rest but given the inheritance of wealth and that wealth is perceived an "unearned", society tends to become more "patrimonial". On the top, privileges are more likely to be passed over to the next generation.

References

Atkinson, Anthony. 2015. *Inequality: What Can Be Done?* Cambridge: Harvard University Press.

Attanasio, Orazio P., and Luigi Pistaferri. 2016. Consumption Inequality. *Journal of Economic Perspectives* 30 (2): 3–28.

Balestra, Carlotta, and Richard Tonkin. 2018. Inequalities in Household Wealth Across OECD Countries: Evidence from the OECD Wealth Distribution Database. OECD Statistics and Data Directorate Working Paper No. 88, 20 June.

Congleton, Roger D., Arye L. Hillman, and Kai A. Konrad. 2008. *40 Years of Research on Rent Seeking*, Vols. 1 and 2. Berlin: Spinger.

Csillag, Tamas, and Iván Szelényi. 2015. Drifting from Liberal Democracy. *Intersection* 1 (1): 1–31.

Darvas, Zsolt. 2016. Some Are More Equal Than Others: New Estimates of Global and Regional Inequality. Bruegel Working Papers, Issue 8.

Deaton, Angus. 2013. *The Great Escape: Health, Wealth, and the Origins of Inequality*. Princeton: Princeton University Press.

Fuest, Clemens, Florian Neumeier, and Daniel Stöhlker. 2018. Why the IMS and OECD Are Wrong About Inequality and Growth. *EconPol Policy Brief* 2, May.

Gimpelson, Vladimir, and Daniel Treisman. 2015. Misperceiving Inequality. NBER Working Papers No. 21174.

Jacobs, Didier. 2015. Extreme Wealth Is Not Merited. Oxfam Discussion Papers, November.

Krueger, Anne O. 1974. The Political Economy of Rent Seeking Society. *American Economic Review* 64 (3): 291–303.

Kuznets, Simon. 1955. Economic Growth and Income Inequality. *American Economic Review* 1: 1–28.

Macrae, Norman. 1983. Into Entrepreneurial Socialism. *The Economist*, March 19, pp. 23–29.

Marx, Karl, and Friedrich Engels. 1848. *Manifesto of the Communist Party*. https://www.marxists.org/archive/marx/works/download/pdf/Manifesto.pdf.

Mihályi, Péter, and Iván Szelényi. 2016a. Two Different Sources of Inequalities: Profits and Rents in Advanced Market Economies. Hungarian Academy of Sciences Discussion Papers, MT-DP—2016/30, August, Institute of Economics, Centre for Economic and Regional Studies.

Mihályi, Péter, and Iván Szelényi. 2016b. Wealth and Capital: A Critique of Piketty's Conceptualisation of Return on Capital. *Cambridge Journal of Economics* (12). December. https://doi.org/10.1093/cje/bew054.

Mihályi, Péter, and Iván Szelényi. 2016c. Az egyenlőtlenségek valódi természetéről [On the True Nature of Inequalities]. *Mozgó Világ*, 11. sz. 3–12 (in Hungarian).

Mihályi, Péter, and Iván Szelényi. 2016d. Járadékvadászat Nyugaton és Keleten [Rent-Seeking in East and West], *168 óra*, No. 31. August 4, pp. 40–41 (in Hungarian).

Mihályi, Péter, and Iván Szelényi. 2017. The Role of Rents in the Transition from Socialist Redistributive Economies to Market Capitalism. *Comparative Sociology* 16: 13–38.

Milanovic, Branko. 2016. *Global Inequality: A New Approach for the Age of Globalization*. Cambridge: Harvard University Press.

OECD. 2015. *In It Together, Why Less Inequality Benefits All*. Paris: OECD Publishing. https://doi.org/10.1787/9789264235120-en.

Ostry, J., A. Berg, and C.G. Tsangarides. 2014. *Redistribution, Inequality, and Growth*. IMF Staff Discussion Note.

Piketty, Thomas, Emmanuel Saez, and Gabriel Zucman. 2016. Economic Growth in the United States: A Tale of Two Countries. Washington Center for Equitable Growth, December. http://equitablegrowth.org/research-analysis/economic-growth-in-the-united-states-a-tale-of-two-countries/.

Posner, Eric A., and E. Glen Weyl. 2018. *Radical Markets Uprooting Capitalism and Democracy for a Just Society*. Princeton: Princeton University Press.

Putnam, Robert D. 2015. *Our Kids: The American Dream in Crisis*. New York: Simon & Schuster.

Solow, Robert. 2015. The Future of Work, Why Wages Aren't Keeping Up? *Pacific Standard*, August 11.

Tóth, István György. 2014. Revisiting Grand Narratives of Growing Income Inequalities: Lessons from 30 Country Studies. In *Changing Inequalities and Societal Impacts in Rich Countries: Thirty Countries' Experiences*, ed. B. Nolan, W. Salverda, D. Checchi, I. Marx, A. Mcknight, I. Gy. Tóth, and H. G. van de Werfhorst, 11–47. Oxford: Oxford University Press.

Tullock, G. 1967. The Welfare Costs of Tariffs, Monopolies and Theft. *Western Economic Journal* 5 (3): 224–232.

Whyte, Martin K. 2010. *Myth of the Social Volcano*. Stanford: Stanford University Press.

World Bank. 2013. *End Extreme Poverty and Promote Shared Prosperity*. Washington, DC: The World Bank. http://www.worldbank.org/content/dam/Worldbank/document/WB-goals2013.pdf.

Zakaria, Fareed. 1997. The Rise of Illiberal Democracy. *Foreign Affairs* 76 (6): 22–43.

CHAPTER 2

Rent in Classical Economic, Social, and Political Theory

Abstract Classics—Locke, Smith, Ricardo, and Marx—struggled with the role labor, capital, and rent play in the determination of prices and incomes. The received wisdom was the labor theory of value: if incomes earned by wage laborers—essentially adult, male breadwinners—are proportional to the value of their labor, the system is fair. If they get less, the laborers are exploited. Few economists would accept this reasoning today, and the authors reject it as well. This chapter brings the views of Max Weber and Aage Sorensen into the discussion of rents in order to build the present book's underlying theory on a solid historical and analytical footing.

Keywords Labor theory of value · Positive- and negative-sum games · Exploitation · Closed and open social relations · Non-capitalist forms of inequalities

1 The Beginning: John Locke and Adam Smith

Classical economic theory from John Locke to Adam Smith, David Ricardo and Karl Marx struggled with the role labor, capital and rent played in the creation of value, and the determination of prices and incomes. The received wisdom in the eighteenth- and the mid-nineteenth-century economics was the **labor theory of value**: if incomes earned

P. Mihályi and I. Szelényi,
Rent-Seekers, Profits, Wages and Inequality,
https://doi.org/10.1007/978-3-030-03846-5_2

by the broad masses of wage laborers—essentially adult, male breadwinners—are proportional to the value of their labor, the system is fair. If they get less, the laborers are exploited. The value of labor is the yardstick, the starting point of comparison. Nothing else really matters beyond labor. Few economists would accept this reasoning today, but the distribution of revenues exclusively between wages and profits is still often a common point of departure in mainstream models (once rents are defined as a part of profits).

John Locke (1632–1704) was an early pioneer of what eventually became the labor theory of value. His argumentation begins with a fascinating point about property rights: "[E]very man has a property in his own person. (...) The labor of his body, and the work of his hand (...) are properly his, Whatsoever then he removes out of the state that nature had provided (...) he had mixed his labor with (...) thereby makes it his property"[1]. It follows: "For this labor being the unquestionable property of the laborer".[2] Finally, with a wonderful turn of offering an irrefutable empirical observation he is ready for the labor theory of value: "Though the water running in the fountain be every ones, yet who can doubt, but that in pitcher is his only who drew it out".[3]

Just a few pages later, we have a full and forceful articulation of the "theory": "Labor [is] indeed that puts differences of value on everything... I think it will be but a very modest computation to say, that of the product of the Earth useful to the life of Man 9/10th are the effects of Labor [with 1/10 attributed to the improvement of land, which of course also occurred due to investment of labor, just at an earlier point in time]".[4]

If that is true, how comes that some who do not offer labor still receive income, rather than all the income a wealth going to the worker? Locke has sophisticated answers. The claim that labor is a source of value is valid only in the "state of nature".

And here we have an early formulation for profit (though the term is not being used): "Invention of money gave them the opportunity to ... enlarge [their property]... What reason could anyone have there to enlarge his possession beyond the use of his Family? But since Gold and

[1] Locke (1698, pp. 287–288).

[2] Locke, ibid., p. 288.

[3] Locke, ibid., p. 289.

[4] Locke, ibid., p. 296.

Silver...has its value ...men have agreed to disproportionate and unequal possession of the Earth... since Gold and Silver can be hoarded up without injury to any one".[5]

In Locke's view, in the state of nature everything is plentiful, especially the fruits of nature and land. Everyone will cultivate only as much land as he needs to feed his/her family, no one will labor for anybody else, since there is ample land to cultivate their own plot. One also cannot store the fruits of land since it will rotten. This stands so until the invention of gold. Locke foreshadows the theory that new value has to be shared among owners of factors of production, owners of labor and capital "agreed" to share the proceeds of produce of labor. Locke, however, does not offer a similar moral–economic justification for rent paid to the owner of land. Rent is not defined as a factor contributing to new value, in this respect, Locke foreshadowed Ricardo and even Henry George.

Adam Smith also used the labor theory of value as his starting point: "The value of any commodity, therefore, to the person who possesses it, and who means not to use or consume it, but to exchange it for other commodities, is equal to the quantity of labor which it enables him to purchase or command... Labor, therefore, is the real measure of the exchangeable value of all commodities. (...) The property which every man has in his own labor, as it is the original foundation of all other property, so it is the most sacred and inviolable".[6]

"In that early (...) society, which precedes both the accumulation of stock [capital] and the appropriation of land, the proportion between the quantities of labor necessary for acquiring different object seems to be the only circumstance which can afford any rule of exchanging them for another. (...) In this state of things, the whole produce of labor belongs to the laborer".[7] "As soon as stock has accumulated in the hands of particular persons, some of them will naturally employ it in setting to work industrious people".[8] And he continues: As soon as land (...) "has become private property the landlord demands a rent".[9] So now we have

[5]Locke, ibid., pp. 301–302.

[6]Adam Smith (1776, Book I, p. 136).

[7]Smith, ibid., pp. 53–54.

[8]Smith, ibid., p. 54.

[9]Smith, ibid., p. 56.

the theory fully elaborated: "**Wages, profit and rent, are the three original sources of all revenue** as well as of all exchangeable value".[10]

He offers a rather persuasive argument (widely accepted by neo-classical economy, supply-side economists) why owners of capital deserve profit: "Owners of capital will (…) employ it in setting to work industrious people. (…) The value the workmen add to the materials (…) resolves itself into two parts (…) one pays their wages, the other the profits. (…) **The profits** (…) may (…) be thought of **only a different name for wages** (…) wages for labor (…) of inspection and direction".[11] Adam Smith nevertheless had a lingering doubt about how much land-ownership contributed to the creation of new wealth: "As soon as land of any country has all become private property, the landlords (…) **love to reap where they never sowed** and demand a rent for its natural produce".[12]

2 Ricardo Was Not Entirely Correct, but…

Ricardo in his first formulation just followed Locke: "On the first settling of a country in which there is abundance of rich and fertile land (…) there will be no rent (…). If all land had the same properties, if it were **unlimited in quantity**, and **uniform in quality**, no charge could be made for its use".[13] Then Ricardo fills the hole left in the theory of Locke and radicalized Smith: "Rent (…) is often (…) confounded with the interest and profit of capital. [L]aws which regulate the progress of rent are widely different from those that regulate the progress of profits, and seldom operate in the same direction (…)".[14] Why are these laws different? Ricardo's answer is trivial: because agricultural land is despairingly scarce. It was always scarce and it will remain scarce as long as humans eat farm products. The supply of land is inelastic, while demand for food steadily grows. Under these circumstances, the owners of land receive scarcity rent without producing more or better food—i.e. without producing new value. Such rents channel resources away from "productive" investments and cuts in real incomes of wage and salary earners.

[10] Smith, ibid., p. 59, our emphasis.

[11] Smith, ibid., p. 55, our emphasis.

[12] Smith, ibid., p. 56, our emphasis.

[13] Ricardo (1817, p. 34), our emphasis.

[14] Ibid., pp. 33–34, our emphasis.

In part, Ricardo proved to be wrong. First, he did not consider how much the fertility of land could be increased. Secondly, he simply didn't know enough about other countries and continents. In retrospect, it is clear that whenever the Homo sapiens needed more land for cultivation, the supply of land turned out to be elastic. Agricultural land could be "produced" by burning down the forests and/or through migration on the mainland.[15] Equally importantly, the price/value of agricultural land declined after the inclusion of the Americas and Australia into the emerging capitalist world economy. In fact, even in the twenty-first century, there is an abundant supply of uncultivated agricultural land around the globe.[16] It is another matter that labor mobility was very limited in his time, therefore English landowners could benefit from their *local* monopoly situation. And that was the big picture Ricardo was familiar with. Modern economists rightly speak of "quasi-rents" to describe payments for services or assets that are inelastically supplied in the short run, but elastically supplied in the long run. Ricardo's case is exactly this.

But Ricardo made a critical distinction between profits/wages and rent and he was entirely right on this. Rent is always the difference between the produce obtained by the employment of two equal quantities of capital and labor. "The price of corn is high not because a rent is paid, but rent is paid because the price of corn is high".[17] "The rise of rent is always the effect of the increasing wealth of the country, and of the difficulty of providing food for its augmented population. **It is a symptom, but it is never the cause of wealth**".[18] While for Locke and Smith wages, profits and rent all contribute to the value and price of the products and to the wealth of the nation, Ricardo only sees such a productive contribution of wages and profits, but rent—at least rent which comes from the (local) scarcity of land—is not the cause of value/price, or wealth, it is the consequence (symptom) of increasing prices/wealth.

Smith and Ricardo were liberals. They advocated capitalist transformation of society. As we will elaborate on the following pages Smith's lingering doubts about and Ricardo's explicit criticism of rent does not follow from the "general logic of capitalism". Ricardo offered a general—not a historically specific—theory, nevertheless it can be

[15] Jones (2015, p. 7).

[16] Under the FAO's definition, agricultural land covers only 33% of the world's land area.

[17] Ricardo, ibid., p. 38.

[18] Ricardo, p. 40, our emphasis.

interpreted as a criticism of landed aristocracy. Ricardo's "scarcity rent" is "unearned" income, which does not contribute to wealth creation, it indeed redistributes incomes from wages and profits into rental revenue. Or to put it differently, while for Locke and Smith wages, profits and rent can be seen as a positive-sum game, Ricardo takes a rather different position. In his theory profit and wage vs. rent is a **negative-sum game**. Since rent does not create new value, it can only come from deduction from profits and/or wages. While thinking and writing mostly about the use of agricultural land, he did mention the relevance of rents for mining and the source of enrichment of mine-owners as well.

Ricardo was the point of departure for Henry George's (1839–1897), an immensely popular American political economist and journalist of his time. He was confronted with the dilemma the United States faced during the late nineteenth century (and what is one of our contemporary major social–political issues). While there is dynamic economic growth, there is substantial poverty and economic inequality. His answer was: rent paid for land, which absorbs the benefits of growth. He went one important step beyond Ricardo; his theory of rent is not limited to land cultivated for agricultural purposes, but also rent collected on urban land ownership. For George, much like for Ricardo this had important implications for taxation policy. Government revenues should come from taxes imposed on rent, because taxes on wages or profits have negative consequences for economic growth. The logical conclusion is a single tax. Tax only rent but not wages or profits, a position is taken by those who are called left-libertarians in the United States even today. With Sorensen's generalization of the theory of rent, our present book comes close to a version of "Georgism" (though as it shall be clear in Chapter 7 we do not believe in a "single tax" system).[19]

3 Karl Marx and His Concept of Exploitation

By 1867 Karl Marx was confronted with a different social world, one of industrial capitalism, so he attempted to frame the "laws of motion" of industrial capitalism—as he knew it. Nevertheless, Marx's point of departure resembled Smith: "The value of each commodity is determined by

[19] Joseph Stiglitz's theory about the relationship between public spending and increase in land rent—called, the Henry George theorem—is a contemporary application of the original idea. See Stiglitz (1977).

the quantity of labor expended on and materialized in it, by the working time necessary, under given social conditions, for its production".[20] But while Smith regarded labor and capital (and at least with some qualification: rents as well) as two independent factors of production, Marx insisted that **capital itself is only accumulated labor**. While for Smith, the critical question was what is the fair distribution of profits, rents, and wages,[21] for Marx, all profits and rents were born form exploitation. We can translate all this into a game theoretic language. For Marx wages vs. profits and rents is a negative-sum game. The right question for him was not to find a better allocation of revenues between wages, profits, and rents, but to eliminate private ownership, which is the sole source of profits and rents. Hence Marx's major innovation is the development of the theory of exploitation.

Marx distinguishes between two types (phases) of the circulation of commodities. Simple circulation of commodities: *C-M-C*. The cycle starts with a commodity produced by the farmer or artisan, which is sold on the market for money (*M*), in order to purchase another commodity which the producer needs. If we use the language of Locke and Smith in "political society" (in latter language of Marx: under "capitalist" relations) there is a second form of circulation of money as capital: *M-C-M'*. This cycle begins with money (*M*) with an exchange value and produces use value in order to obtain more money (*M'*). The purpose of production is not satisfaction of human needs, but maximization of profit (and rent)—the original sin of capitalism for Marx.

Marx's great project was to offer a scientific explanation why capitalism will have to collapse. Does the "theory of exploitation" achieve this aim? It does not. Instead, Volume I of *Capital*—Marx's arguably most important and entirely completed book, which came out first in 1867—presented an equilibrium theory of the capitalist economy. In fact, this book was better suited to explain the iron law of reproduction of capitalism, the "satanic mills"[22]—rather than its inevitable collapse. How comes?

[20] Marx. *Capital* ([1867] 1954, p. 208).

[21] This was still the typical question of the twentieth-century social democrats and trade unionist, who fought for higher wages and lower profits and rents.

[22] The term "satanic mills" was coined by William Blake (1757–1827), a radical Christian poet. In a poem, he wrote around 1810 he used the term, as a criticism of orthodox churches. At one later point in time, Gramscian Marxists who emphasized the tendency of capitalism to reproduce itself adopted this metaphor as a description of capitalist

The initial big puzzle is where *M'* does come from? For Marx, Proudhon's proposition that "private property is theft"[23] was far too simplistic and ideological. In order to have a scientific—rather than ideological—theory of capitalist production one needed the following assumption: "The conversion of money into capital has to be explained on the basis of laws that regulate the exchange of commodities, in such a way that the starting point is the **exchange of equivalents**".[24] The paradox is here: at the end of the production process, the capitalist must have more capital than it had when the production cycle began. In his own model, Marx had to find answers to two questions. (i) If we have to assume that always equivalents have to be exchanged (no one cheats nobody[25]), how can this miracle of gaining more money at the end of the cycle occur? (ii) What can and has to do the capitalist with capital thus accumulated?

For the first question, Marx offers an elegant though somewhat Talmudist explanation: a sharp distinction between labor and labor power. What the laborer sells, according to Marx, is not his labor, but his/her labor power. The price of labor power is the same as the price of any other commodity: hence the costs of its reproduction. The value of labor power "is the value of the means of subsistence necessary for the maintenance of the laborer".[26] The trick is that labor power is the only commodity, which produces more value than its own value when consumed. The worker can produce enough value in x hours to cover the costs of reproduction of his labor power (which even includes the costs of production of the next generation of workers, the costs of raising his/her children), but since his/her labor power is now under the control of the capitalist, the capitalist will require the worker to work $x + y$ hours. Could the capitalist pay *less* to the workers than the value generated during x hours? No, since in this case the worker will not be able to

reproduction unless revolutionary consciousness overcomes the over-determination of the capitalist mode of production, see Burawoy (1984).

[23]This slogan (In French: *La propriété, c'est le vol!*) was coined by the French anarchist Pierre-Joseph Proudhon (1809–1865) in his 1840 book *What is Property? Or, an Inquiry into the Principle of Right and of Government.*

[24]Marx, ibid., p. 161, our emphasis.

[25]Marx, ibid., p. 161.

[26]Marx, ibid., p. 190.

keep producing itself and the working class will starve. Could it pay the worker *more* than, share some of the value created working hours *y*? (To be a "generous" capitalist?) No, since in this case, the worker will start accumulating capital, will eventually become a capitalist and stop selling his/her labor power.

But this leads Marx to the second question. What will the capitalist now do with *M'*? Capitalists compete with each other. If a capitalist would be foolish enough not to invest into expanded production, he will be wiped out by competition. This is indeed the mechanism of the "satanic mills", mentioned earlier. The worker, derived from the means of subsistence has to sell his/her labor power, cannot collect less or more than the costs of reproduction of this/her labor power and the capitalist has no choice but to use the profit (called surplus by Marx) expropriated from their workers to reinvest, expand production and/or improve productivity. Marx was searching for a scientific theory to explain why capitalism has to fall, but if we eliminate the heated language he used ("money bags"), the exploitation theory of Volume I only explains why capitalism will never fall.

During the 1980s there emerged a new trend in Marxism, which fundamentally rejected the early Marx (such as his theory of alienation) as "Bullshit-Marxism" and relied heavily on rational choice theory to make Marxism "scientific" enough. Marx indeed in his later work—especially in *The Capital*—offered a tight rational argument to explain the functioning of the "idealized" model of capitalism, as he knew it, and as he expected to develop in the future—i.e. British capitalism of the nineteenth century. Scholars like John Roemer, E. O. Wright, Jon Elster or Adam Przeworski relied heavily on the "scientific" Marx and their interpretation of Marx is rather similar to neo-classical economics and rational choice theory (it is another question whether the later work of Elster or Przeworski will be accepted as "Marxist" by other Marxists).[27]

In the third volume of *The Capital*, which he never actually completed, Marx made an effort to find the scientific proof for the fall of capitalism. He formulated another fascinating, but logically incomplete and empirically dubious hypothesis of the "tendency of the rate of profit to decline"—an idea, which had been already contemplated by Ricardo

[27] The term idealized in the previous sentence is important. As we know, the major shortcoming of neo-classical economics is that there are no perfect markets in any "actually existing" capitalist economies.

at the very beginning of his grand *oeuvre*. Marx was aware that there are "counteracting tendencies" (though surprisingly he did not elaborate on the most important "counteracting tendency": namely that productivity increase from technological innovations can be far greater than the costs of investment into constant capital). So, he left the manuscript unpublished and it was Engels who turned the declining rate of profits into a "law" which explains the inevitability of the demise of the capitalist mode of production.

In our reading, since Marx could not persuade himself that he really found the scientific theory he was looking for, he turned his attention to ground rent. While for Ricardo rent for landed property was distinctly different from capitalist profits, Marx's lengthy and somewhat difficult to digest elaboration on rent wanted to understand rent as a feature of market capitalism, just another form of profit.[28] Nevertheless much to his to horror in Chapter 52 of Volume III, he suddenly realized that he is back at Adam Smith: "The owners merely of labor- power, owners of capital, and landowners (…) constitute then three big classes of modern society based upon the capitalist mode of production".[29] The powerful two-class model of bourgeoisie vs. proletariat is now replaced with a three-class model, where wages, profits, and rents are just three different sources of income, hence the inherent equilibrium tendency of the exploitation theory is not resolved. Marx finishes the page and breaks the manuscript off and left Volumes II and III "to the gnawing criticism of the mice".[30] We believe that Marx moved in the wrong direction and lost the important insights Ricardo had offered about the differences between profits and rents.

As we said already, in a closed economy, under perfect competition, the individual capitalist has no choice. He has to keep wages at the level of reproduction of the labor power and limit his own consumption, because he needs to reinvest his profit in order to remain competitive with other capitalists. As John Maynard Keynes noted in a not very frequently quoted passage of his otherwise widely celebrated book of 1920, *The Economic Consequences of The Peace*, the capitalists of the

[28] See, especially Marx, pp. 773–774, 782–783.

[29] Ibid., p. 885.

[30] Marx wrote this about the German Ideology in *A Contribution to the Critique of Political Economy* (1857), but it is reasonable to assume that he found Volume II and III equally incomplete, not ready to be printed. It is especially telling the Volume III, Chapter 52, which was supposed to be the grand conclusion is broken off on the second page.

late nineteenth century "were allowed to call the best part of the cake theirs, and were theoretically free to consume it, on the tacit underlying condition that they consumed very little of it in practice".[31] Hence, under such circumstances, the expanded reproduction process appeared to Keynes as a positive-sum game. Five decades earlier, Karl Marx had also thought in that way, although he did not use this game-theory metaphor. If almost the entire amount of profit had to be reinvested, more profits—*ceteris paribus*—meant more jobs, or in tight labor markets, higher wages.[32]

4 Closed and Open Social Relations, Rent-Seeking and Profit-Seeking Activity: Max Weber

Max Weber (1864–1921) made a captivating distinction between "open" and "closed" relationships. As most Weberian concepts this is in part historical, in part analytical. History tends to move from more closed to more open relations, but even in contemporary societies, closed and open relations co-exists and necessarily complement each other. "Social relationship (…) will be spoken as 'open' to outsiders if and insofar as its system of order does not deny participation to anyone who wishes to join and is actually in a position to do so.[33] A relationship will (…) be called 'closed' against outsiders so far as (…) participation of certain persons is excluded, limited or subjected to conditions".[34]

At first sight, the Weberian concept of "closed" and "open" relationships looks identical to the proposition in Acemoglu and Robinson (2012), who coined the terms "*exclusive*" and "*inclusive*" societies. But the two are not the same. The American authors—as the title of their book emphasizes—analyze the growth process at the level of nations. Weber speaks of "closed" and "open" relationships also at the level of nations, but at the same time he uses the concept also within a given

[31] Keynes ([1920] 1971, p. 20).

[32] Although Marx himself didn't consider such an option, higher profits could also finance higher wages for workers in order to generate sufficient demand for capitalist production.

[33] This is a very interesting qualification. Weber tries to avoid the Marxian trap, namely that workers since they do not have capital by definition cannot enter competition. Both capitalist and workers compete: workers with workers, capitalists with capitalists.

[34] Weber (1978, p. 43).

economy for organization or groups of population[35]—and this is the right approach, if we analyze inequalities within a given country. The same can be said about the dual concept of "*open and limited access orders*" presented in North et al. (2012). Nevertheless, we strongly agree with all these authors concerning the ubiquitous presence of rent in every society, including the most advanced countries.

Weber's distinction between open and close relations is tightly connected to the distinction between profit and rent, capital and wealth. "This distinction between private wealth and capital, between the budgetary unit and the profit-making enterprise is of far-reaching importance. In particular, without it, it is impossible to understand the economic development of the ancient world and the limitation on the development of the capitalism of those times". So he continues: "[T]he 'profit-making enterprise' will be confined to those type of acquisitive activity which is continually oriented to market advantages. (…) The person who is a mere rentier or investor of private wealth (…) is not engaged in profit making, no matter how rationally he administers his resources".[36]

5 Various Non-capitalist Forms of Inequalities and Exploitation

Unlike Piketty, we do not believe that the largest part of present-day inequalities can be derived from the "fundamental laws of capitalism".[37] But before we dwell upon our interpretation of rent in modern, advanced capitalist countries, as the main source of certain type of inequalities, we make four clarifications pertaining to the past and current *levels* of inequality which do not originate in the logic of free-market rivalry and the invisible hand of the capitalist market economies.

(i) Pre-capitalist societies were brutally unequal, but they functioned in ways different from the textbook ownership models of the nineteenth- and twentieth-century "classical" capitalism. The rulers and the top 1–10% of the society lived from the food surplus of

[35] For instance kinship, caste, or estate can be characterized by close relations, while classes or occupational groups are open.

[36] Max Weber (1978, Volume I, p. 99).

[37] Stiglitz (2015b) makes similar comments on Piketty's book (p. 428, 444).

> the peasants and did not leave more to them than the subsistence minimum for biological survival. This type of inequity of power and wealth, suppression and discrimination were based almost exclusively on social rank/estate (what Max Weber called *Stand*) or racial, ethnic, and caste divisions. All of these positions tended to be **hereditary** or to put it differently based on ascription, rather than achievement. As societies transitioned into classical capitalism and inequalities emerged more and more on market positions, certain pre-capitalist exploitation forms were carried over into the early phases of capitalism in many countries. In England, for example, the nobility—i.e. the landlords—enclosed the commons and turned themselves into capitalists from the thirteenth century onwards. In many underdeveloped countries, this type of transition is still ongoing.

During the second half of the twentieth century, the autocratic leaders of some socialist countries desperately tried to extend their personal political power to their close relatives (Kim Jong-il in North Korea, Fidel Castro in Cuba, Nicolae Ceaușescu in Romania, Todor Zhivkov in Bulgaria and Eric Honecker in the German Democratic Republic, etc.). Even today, one can still find unelected traditional rulers and their entire dynasties on the very top of the social ladder, such as the sheikhs of the Gulf States, the kings and tribal chiefs of many African countries owning the most valuable modern capital assets of their respective countries. In countries like India, Bangladesh, or Greece the positions of elected political leaders—prime ministers and presidents—have been captured by certain families for two or three generations.

Furthermore, ethno-racial, religious, gender-based, urban–rural, and political discriminations are *still* major drivers of visible and measurable relative poverty. Consider the situation of African-Americans or Native-Americans in the United States, the fate of Aborigines in Australia, the misery of indigenous people in some Latin American countries, the suppression of Muslims by Hindus, Shiites by Sunnites (or vice versa), the unfolding tragedy of the Rohingya people in Myanmar, etc. Other types of pre-capitalist social categorizations remain also highly consequential, like the caste of untouchables in India and Japan, or in Kazakhstan, where the entire population is "ranked" in three clans or *jüz* in Kazakh. An interesting, non-capitalist form of discrimination based on family-tied political loyalty was upheld in Bangladesh for decades. The ruling Awami

League, which led the country's independence movement, reserved 30% of public posts for descendants of those who fought in the war of secession from Pakistan in 1971—almost 50 years ago![38]

In small pockets of the world, even slavery continues to exist: people forced to work in agriculture, domestic work and factories. Entire families forced to work for nothing to pay off generational debts. Their total number is estimated at 40 million.[39] In East European countries, especially in Bulgaria, Hungary, Macedonia, Romania, Serbia, and Slovakia, the Roma (gipsy) population is discriminated. The exclusion of a significant percentage of this large Roma population explains a good part of the inequalities, as measured at the national level by the usual indicators (e.g. Gini coefficient, absolute poverty).[40]

In China, Beijing and many other cities treat settlers from other parts of the same country as second-class citizens preventing them to benefit from the "blessings" of metropolitan life. This is the consequence of the *hukou* system, which ties hundreds of millions of Chinese to the place their family came from—essentially the rural areas. Similar institutions exist in some other Asian countries, as well.[41] In the Soviet Union, the *Propiska* system worked precisely in the same way from 1932 until the collapse of the communist regime.

(ii) In the realm of **reproductive success**, huge inequalities have existed since the dawn of modern humans. Some males end up having lots of children with different women, while a significant number of males end up having none at all, e.g. in the newly independent state of South Sudan with a population of 12 million, it is estimated that 40% of marriages are polygamous. Every time a rich man takes an extra wife, a poor man must remain

[38]This system was only recently abolished after massive anti-government rallies. See *The Economist*, April 21, 2018.

[39]https://www.antislavery.org/slavery-today/modern-slavery/.

[40]According to the last estimates made by the Council of Europe, the share of Roma in the above-mentioned six countries ranges from 6.8 to 10.3%. The exact share of this minority in the population (and the very definition who are Roma) is hotly debated.

[41]Although the *hukou* system has origins in China dating back to ancient times, the system in its current form came into being with the 1958 People's Republic of China Hukou Registration Regulation. In present times, a similar household registration system exists within the public administration structures of Japan (*koseki*), Vietnam (*hộ khẩu*), and North Korea (*hoju*). In South Korea, the *hoju* system was abolished on 1 January 2008.

> single—simply because the relative supply of marriageable women is fixed at a given point in time. If the wealthiest 10% of man have, say, four wives each, the bottom 30% cannot marry. South Sudan is not a very special exception. Although in most countries polygamy is illegal, it is estimated that more than a third of women in West Africa are married to a man who has more wives. Plural marriages *de facto* (even *de jure*) exist in many Arab countries, in Southeast Asia and a few parts of the Caribbean.[42] Child marriage and sexual harassment of women—a sensational topic of the year 2017—are less brutal forms of exploitation, but they also predate capitalism by thousands of years.

Inequalities within nuclear families need to be mentioned also, such as the fate of "missing women" and "unwanted girls" in China and many parts of Southeast Asia and North Africa. The term "missing women", first used in India, indicates a shortfall in the number of women relative to the expected number of women in a region or country. It is most often measured through male-to-female sex ratios, as a result of sex-selective abortions, female infanticide, and inadequate health care and nutrition for female children.[43] The category of unwanted—and often neglected—girls refer to the practice, according to which poor, rural Indian families continue to produce children until a boy is born. After that, the daughters born earlier are treated as second-class children throughout their early childhood—with predictable consequences in their later life. Until 2005, when the Hindu inheritance law was substantially reformed, the discrimination continued with full force into adulthood as well. In other parts of the world, hundreds of millions of Muslim grown-up women are still legally discriminated vis-à-vis their brothers according to the Islamic sharia law of inheritance: the share of the male is twice that of a female. In many countries, even the boys are not equal. The principle of primogeniture negatively affects all the other males; the eldest son inherits all of the family property (or a disproportionally large share), e.g. in South Korea, favoring the eldest son has been predominant almost up to recent times, despite laws of equal inheritance for all children.

[42] *The Economist*, 23 December 2017, pp. 26–28.

[43] See the seminal works of Sen (1990, 1992).

(iii) While inequalities are obviously reflected in **health outcomes** at the society level, ill-health in itself is an independent source of injustice even in the most advanced countries. As a result of genetic heritage, a fatal accident or infection (e.g. AIDS) many people lose partly or fully their wage-earning capabilities for a prolonged period, or forever. This and the uncompensated, above-average health expenditures are likely to prohibit these people to accumulate wealth in line with their social peers. This does not have much to do with the political economy of capitalism, either.

(iv) The existence of smaller or larger inequalities in incomes is often merely a reflection of the state-created, statutory **minimum wage** system—if there is such an institution. Advanced, industrialized market economies use this social institution widely, poor countries rarely. It is noteworthy, however, that minimum wages, as a percentage of the median-wage vary significantly even among the developed countries. In 2016, the legislated minimum wage among the OECD countries amounted to 61% of the average wages of full-time workers in France, but only 49 and 35% in the UK and the United States, respectively.[44] These widely different proportions are not determined by economic "laws"—they are simply the result of accidental changes shaping the local labor markets through decades. Furthermore, there is a trade-off between higher wage inequality and the level of underemployment among the businesswise less efficient potential workers. When wages are not subject to state control from the bottom, it is much easier to find work for the disprivileged—the underskilled, the ethnic minorities, the migrants, the very old and the young school-leavers, as well as people with pre-existing health disparities.

* * *

After this detour into the present-day examples of the non-capitalist forms of inequalities, let us continue our overview of the different rent theories with Max Weber's analysis. We know from him that in

[44]https://stats.oecd.org/Index.aspx?DataSetCode=MIN2AVE, accessed on 9 August 2018.

pre-capitalist, agrarian economies the dominant form of socio-economic organization is based on closed social relations. Economically speaking the system is centered around the "household" economy (*oikos*), which operates as a budgetary unit. The feudal landlord's or the slave owner's revenue is rent, the prime examples of revenue stemming from closed social relationships. Feudal landlords and slave owners "are typically rentiers", who extract products of labor or labor services from serves and slaves and in exchange guarantee their subsistence (slaves and serfs typically do not earn wages, just have the right to grow their own food, or are being fed/closed/housed by the lord or master). The "surplus value" extracted this way is typically not reinvested for profit maximization purposes, but instead, it supports the usually luxurious lifestyles of the court or household of the landlords or slave-owning masters.

Max Weber's distinction between private wealth, operating as landed estates, as *oikos*, budgetary units and capital, the profit-making enterprise, is of far-reaching importance. As long as the economy is dominated by landed estates, budgetary accounting—as was the case in the Ancient world and under Western feudalism (and to some extent under state socialism) the development of the capitalism and dynamic economic growth was greatly limited. "*The person who is a mere rentier (…) is (…) not engaged in profit making*"[45] and without an economy dominated by profit-making enterprises the economy will be stagnant. Even the Medieval urban economies in the ocean of rural countryside followed a similar logic: Trade and artisanship were organized by guilds, a strictly closed organization. Entering a guild was an arduous and highly selective process, which may lasted for many years (ridiculously long apprenticeship) and could depend on family connections. Guild member's revenue though can be conceptualized as composed of wages/profit + rent. Most guild members (remember Hans Sachs in *Meistersinger*?) physically produced goods (and earned a "wage" for it), run a business (exploited or even abused their apprentices, collected profits from their work), but since they monopolized the trade, they undoubtedly sold their products over the free-market determined price, hence they collected rent.

So is it only land or real estate from which such rent can stem? As the example of the guilds shows—obviously not. According to Weber, closed groups manage to monopolize advantages to their party, by occupying

[45] Op. cit., p. 99.

scarce and desirable positions, or by making desirable goods and services scarce through clientelist practices, by the creation of cartels, oligopolies or monopolies.[46] Hence it is quite clear for Weber that rent-seeking and profit maximization are two radically different activities, the first occurs in "closed relationships"—like in pre-capitalist societies, or in a monopolistic environment, the second on open competition in market economies. For Weber rent is not just ground rent, but "income derived from the exploitation over important means of production" including those from political authority, monopolies, etc.[47]

Today, such rent is one of the explanations of the very high compensation packages offered to the best specialists.[48] Firms, as well as universities, hospitals, sports clubs, etc. compete with their peers for stars. They don't want to lose a legendary CEO, a professor or an athlete to their rivals. It would hurt their prestige and profits. Therefore, they pay more and more, especially in those countries where excessively progressive income taxes do not counterbalance such incentives.

While the received wisdom from Kuznets (1955) to Piketty (2014) is that inequalities were modest in the early stages of development, they increased with industrialization and then began to decline later (this is the inverted U-curve of Kuznets) nevertheless, many economists and sociologists, including Piketty detected the re-emergence of inequality after the 1970s. We do not have reliable data for pre-capitalist times, but it is safe to assume, that the nature of inequality before capitalism was of different kind (mainly driven by rent rather than by profit) and its extent was substantially higher (and more rigid) than under capitalism. **Class inequality under the worst case of capitalism must have been trivial in comparison with inequalities between slave owners and slaves, landlords, and serfs**. Now, let us make a brief remark on **socialism**. In communist ideology, socialism was usually defined as a transition stage between advanced capitalism to communism. This proved to be historically/empirically incorrect. Socialism was rather a transition from feudalism to capitalism. Workers under socialism were neither slaves nor servants, but they were not wage laborers either, selling their labor power on competitive labor markets. They operated in rather "closed"

[46] See Weber (1921, pp. 43–44). Clearly, all this is very close to the concept of Acemoglu and Robinson (2012).

[47] Op. cit., p. 204.

[48] Solow (2014) calls this rent of supermanagers a "sort of adjunct to capital".

social relations, they were not free to decide whether they work or not, they could not negotiate their wages. Under these circumstances, there was little if any relationship between their productivity and remuneration. Neither employers nor employees were actors on the labor market. In classical socialism, labor was allocated on a non-market trade of labor, to put it with Karl Polanyi (1957). Under socialism, social relations were not class relations but rather relations among status groups. Actors were slotted into the hierarchy of status groups according to three credentials (education, party membership and position in the *nomenclature*) and incomes were centrally controlled and defined accordingly.[49]

"Public ownership" while in part was fictional had a rational element. Since the socialist economy was an economy of shortage (Kornai 1980), not only full employment was guaranteed, but all positions from unskilled workers to top management were practically "tenured". Once you entered a status group (*Stand*) you could not be fired, you had a chance to be promoted to be a higher status group if you received new credentials or were admitted to an in-group, like you joined the communist party. The employed worker or manager had de facto property right in the assets of the firm/organization where they were employed and as proprietors they collected a "rent", even if they did not contribute anything to the productivity of the firm/organization. What one received over that minimum in his/her status group could be seen as wage or profit (with the qualification that given the semi-feudal/socialist character of the system this higher income did not necessarily reflect greater contribution to productivity, but might have been a reward for loyalty—hence a special form of rent[50]). We know little about the true extent of inequality under socialism. In most scholarly writing it is probably underestimated since fringe benefits were not taken into consideration, but socialist economies were relatively egalitarian (more so than feudal or most capitalist economies). In terms of the logic of inequality, they were closer to pre capitalist formations than to market capitalism.

[49]Kornai (1992, pp. 216–227).

[50]In Roemer (1982) book, written at a time, when socialism was an existing and strong political system, this reward for political loyalty in the socialist countries was named "status exploitation" by him. We hope that our readers will agree with us, that it makes much more sense to call this kind of income "rent", rather than getting into the logical trouble to explain who is exploiting whom. Op. cit., pp. 243–247.

6 Interpretation and Generalization of Ricardo's Theory of Rent by Sorensen

Some contemporary economists, in particular, Joseph Stiglitz, the recipient of the Nobel Memorial Prize of 2001, began to formulate a border notion of rent: it is no longer reduced to income collected for land ownership or ownership of natural resources. In Stiglitz formulation: "Much of inequality that exists today is a result of government policy". Our political system has increasingly worked in ways that increase the inequality of outcomes and reduces of equality of opportunity: "(The) political system (…) gives inordinate power to those on the top… to extract from the public what can only be called 'gifts'. Economists have a name for these activities: they call them rent seeking".[51] And he continues, very much along the lines of Ricardo: "(There) are two ways to become wealthy: to create wealth or to take away wealth from others. The former adds to society. The latter subtracts from it (…). A monopolist who overcharges for his product takes money from those whom he is overcharging. (Even) genuine wealth creators often are not satisfied with the wealth that their innovation or entrepreneurship has reaped. Some eventually turn to abusive practices like monopoly pricing or other forms of rent extraction".[52] For Stiglitz therefore rent is not just ground rent, it is income which is earned above income what one could attain on competitive market due to monopolies, cartels or state clientelism.

Aage Sorensen (2000) in his path-breaking article generalizes Ricardo's theory of rent.[53] The Sorensen article was cast as a debate with Erik Olin Wright's class theory. Wright (1985) in the classical traditions of Marxist theory conceptualizes exploitation—as the basis of fundamental class division—between profits and wages. In this interpretation of Marx, profits vs. wages is a negative-sum game, what capitalists gain the workers lose, hence their relationship is antagonistic and will eventually lead to a revolutionary overthrow of the capitalist order. In contrast, Sorensen sees rents vs. (profits + wages) as a negative-sum game where he defines rent as income stemming from closed relationships (in the Weberian sense of the term), hence as income which is higher than the income would be in perfectly competitive markets (as neo-classical

[51] Stiglitz (2012, pp. 15–39).

[52] Op. cit., p. 40.

[53] For a comprehensive overview of Sorensen's work see Trond Petersen (2004).

economists would put it). Sorensen calls such rental income exploitation (Stiglitz also uses the term "exploitation rent"[54]) and sees it as a measure of class divisions.

Though we do not follow Sorensen in his attempt to offer a new theory of exploitation or class we find his definition of rent intriguing: "Rents are payments to assets that exceed the competitive price or the price sufficient to cover costs and therefore exceeding what is sufficient to bring about the employment of the asset". The existence of rent depends on the ability of the owner of the asset to control supply.

Rent is a component of what ordinarily called profit, but profit as usually calculated includes a payment to capital, or interest, earned as payment for past savings and a component of wage to the owner of the asset for his management of asset. The latter components are not part of the rent received when interest and wages equal to market rates of return.[55]

Sorensen made a distinction between three types of rent:

- monopoly rent,
- composite rent, and
- rent based on natural abilities and talents.[56]

Here is his intriguing definition of monopoly rent: "(S)ocial constraints on production create monopoly rents. The monopoly rent (1) may have emerged 'naturally' because of increasing returns to scale creating prohibitive costs of entering production by others. (2) Often monopolies are created by governments as licenses or patents. (…) (3) (S)ocial associations such as trade unions or industry associations, who agree to regulate the production of something, create monopolies".[57] "A special case of monopoly rent is employment rent. On this case employment/jobs are closed to outsiders by the collective action of unions, by government approved certification of professions".[58] We find his first and second definition very interesting and persuasive: the source of monopoly rent can stem from the (mal)functioning of market (excessive accumulation of capital which prohibits new entrants to enter the market and hence

[54] Stiglitz (2015b, p. 425).

[55] Sorensen (2000, p. 1536).

[56] p. 1542.

[57] p. 1542.

[58] pp. 1545–1546.

reduces competition), or it can be government intervention. Sorensen reduces those to licenses and patients and does not even consider what we will call state capture of markets, hence the situation when the state regulates who can enter competition, it allows only clients to compete and excludes those who are non-loyal to political powers. Later in the book, we will suggest that licenses and patients are less likely to block economic growth and threaten social peace, but state clientelism (more widespread in post-communist economies) is likely to do it. [59]

As we have shown above, Sorensen added two more types of rents: composite rent and rents on natural and cultural endowments: "When two separate assets (…) (if jointly used) exceeds the payment to each resource in separate use composite rent emerges".[60] Examples are on the job training (excluding the transfer of skills from one organization to another—what can be seen as "deskilling" by those with formal qualification) and promotion systems within an organization. Within that organization, this can increase both profits and wages, at the expense of profits and wages outside this organization. Furthermore, rents may emerge "on free gifts of nature in the form of genetic endowments that results in the ability to produce something in demand. The rents directly reflect genetic endowments, as when genes are responsible for certain physical attributes facilitating certain tasks, for example, the height for baseball players. Or the rents obtain indirectly when an individual endowment facilitates training for certain skills, as in academic achievement" (hence "cultural capital" *á la* Bourdieu in upper middle class families of Ivy League education).[61]

It is not clear whether these two types of incomes are really "rent". Arguably people—with exceptional physical capabilities—and that may be genetically defined—often earn very high incomes. But they earn these incomes as exceptional football players (they tend to be tall and strong) or economics professors (they are assumed to be especially

[59] Stiglitz offers a similar analysis with his concept of "exploitation rent". He attributes rent to either monopolies or political influence (p. 432). Both Sorensen and Stiglitz, however, operate with the assumption, that free competition is a solution to rent-seeking. But some theorists, most recently Akerlof and Shiller (2015) reminds us that even under "perfect" market competition rent can be generated, by deception of consumers (phishing for phools).

[60] Ibid.

[61] p. 1547.

smart) since their skills are sought after on competitive markets hence their high income is salary and not rent.

Inequality stemming from profits vs. wages is a moral/political problem.[62] We do not underestimate the importance of these inequalities—in each liberal democracy given the value system of the society the citizens decide how much inequality is acceptable and how much income or wealth from the rich shall be redistributed through taxation to the poor. But inequalities from rents originating from closed relations pose unique challenges: (i) a legitimation problem of liberal capitalism, which claims to be meritocratic; and (ii) more importantly, they may undermine the most effective allocation of resources.[63] Mancur Olson (1982) already described historical instances when rent-seeking behavior, which captured state regulations or licensing, led to state collapses. To repeat it provocatively: in open social relations (perfectly competitive markets) as long as the sum of profits + wages is growing, this is a positive-sum game for the society. If rents are growing faster than the sum of profits + wages, this is a negative-sum game. In this regard, we fully agree with Stiglitz (2012).[64]

So far, we described the Weberian distinction between closed and open relations in historical terms, but as we already pointed out it is also an analytic one. Weber does acknowledge—much like Adam Smith does—that in modern capitalist economies' incomes come from three different sources: wages, profits, and rents.[65] His evaluation of the three sources is the most interesting one: "Of all types of incomes, it is particularly those from business profits and the contracted piece rate or free labor incomes which have a dynamic, revolutionary significance for economic life. Next to these stand incomes derived from free exchange and, in quite different

[62] Stiglitz also emphasizes, that inequality not stemming from the logic of capitalism, is a political problem (2015b, p. 444).

[63] Or saying the same in a more modest way: in an economy thoroughly permeated with rents, there is no mechanism which guarantees the most efficient use of assets.

[64] "In the aftermath of the financial crisis, no one today would argue that the banker's pursuit of their self-interest has led to the well- being of all. At most, it led to the banker's well-being... It was a negative--sum game, where the gains for winners are less than the losses to the losers. What the rest of society lost was far greater than the banker's payoff.... When the market works well – in the way Adam Smith hypothesized - it is because private returns and social benefits are aligned..." p. 41.

[65] Weber (1978, p. 205).

ways, under certain circumstances the 'predatory' incomes. Those having a static, conservative influence on economic activity are above all incomes drawn in accordance with a predetermined scale, namely salaries, wages reckoned per unit of working time, gains from exploitation of office powers, and normally all kinds of fixed interest and rents".[66]

It is fascinating that these comments by Weber remind Guenther Roth (1978)—one of the best Weber scholars—of Wilfredo Pareto (1848–1923), the Italian sociologist, economist, political scientist, and philosopher.[67] Pareto in his *The Mind and Society* made an interesting distinction between "speculators" (foxes) and "rentiers" (lions), hence between those who seek profits and those who seek rent. A balanced market capitalist economy needs both foxes and lions; dynamism and innovation have to be counterbalanced by stability. Hence, the proper question is not how much wages/profits vs. rent, but how much of what kinds of wages/profits vs. how much and what kind of rents. If some sorts of foxes are too many it may damage the health of the economy, but the same goes for certain types and certain number of lions. Weber indeed seems to be deeply influenced by this idea of balance between foxes and lions, dynamism and stability, profits and rents.

Rent-seeking creates a different kind of inequality than profit maximization and calls for different policy responses. In our reading, Piketty's most innovative contribution in his "*Capital in the 21st century*" is exactly that he is warning about the transformation of modern capitalism into patrimonial system. This, in our reading, implies the growing proportion of high incomes and wealth from inheritance. These inequalities are coming from rent, based on monopoly or cartel rather than profits or wages. All this is consistent with the friendly amendments Stiglitz (2015a, I, II, III) and Atkinson (2015) made to the Piketty book. In other words, **capitalism in the late twentieth and early twenty-first centuries becomes unequal in a different way: more and more wealth (and privileged social position) is inherited**. Table 1 gives a summary of our historical categorization of rent theories presented in this chapter.

[66] Weber (1978, p. 205).

[67] See Footnote 44, Weber (1978, p. 211).

Table 1 An overview of rent theories

	Smith	*Ricardo*	*Marx*	*Stiglitz*	*Sorensen*	*Piketty*
Source of inequality	Free competition reduces inequality of feudal privileges	Scarcity of agrarian land and mines produces rent	Profit for owners of capital, wages for owners of labor power	Profit for owners of capital and rents for owners of scarce resources	Control over supply by ownership of scarce assets leads to rent	Return on capital (r) (profit + rent)
Market competition	Perfect	Competition for scarce land is limited	Perfect	Imperfect information and imperfect competition	Perfect competition for profits vs. wages, imperfect competition for rent	Perfect competition, except for inherited capital/wealth
Labor theory of value	Accepted			Rejected		
Marginal productivity theory of income distribution	Not known			Accepts it as a good approximation, by noting that it has become less and less applicable in the last 30 years	Rejected	Accepts it as a general rule, but notes that it is less and less applicable to the top 1.0% (e.g. supermanagers)
Social classes	Three non-antagonistic classes based on ownership of factors of production: labor, capital, and land		Two antagonistic classes based on relations of production owners of capital vs. proletariat	Non-antagonistic classes based on distribution of income, upper class, middle class, and lower class	Antagonistic classes, owners of scarce assets are exploiters, those who do not collect rent are exploited	Three non-antagonistic classes based on distribution of income, (upper, middle, and lower), but antagonism between rent-seekers and the rest of the society
Future of capitalism	Radiant	May be destroyed as scarcity rent is increasing	Declining rate of profit and the revolution of the proletariat will destroy capitalism in the most advanced countries	Progressive taxes on incomes and taxes of rent-generating wealth may save capitalism	No prediction	Without a global reform of taxation meritocratic, capitalism will become rent-seeking patrimonial capitalism

References

Acemoglu, D., and J. Robinson. 2012. *Why Nations Fail: The Origins of Power, Prosperity, and Poverty*. Boston: Harvard University Press.

Akerlof, George, and Robert Shiller. 2015. *Phishing for Phools: The Economics of Manipulation and Deception*. Princeton: Princeton University Press.

Atkinson, Anthony. 2015. *Inequality: What Can Be Done?* Cambridge: Harvard University Press.

Burawoy, Michael. 1984. Karl Marx and the Satanic Mills: Factory Politics Under Early Capitalism in England and the United States. *American Journal of Sociology* 90 (2): 247–282.

Jones, Charles I. 2015. The Facts of Economic Growth. NBER Working Paper Series, 21142, May.

Keynes, J. Maynard. [1920] 1971. *The Economic Consequences of the Peace*. New York: Harper Torchbooks.

Kornai, János. 1980. *Economics of Shortage*. Amsterdam: North Holland Publishers.

Kornai, János. 1992. *The Socialist System*. Princeton: Princeton University Press.

Kuznets, Simon. 1955. Economic Growth and Income Inequality. *American Economic Review* 1: 1–28.

Locke, John. [1698] 1988. *Two Treatise of Governmen*t. Cambridge: Cambridge University Press.

Marx, Karl. [1867] 1954. *Capital: A Critique of Political Economy*. Moscow: Progress Publisher.

North, Duglas, John Joseph Wallis, Steven B. Webbs, and Berry Weinsgast. [2009] 2012. *Violence and Social Order*. Cambridge: Cambridge University Press.

Olson, Mancur. 1982. *The Rise and Decline of Nations*. New Haven, CT: Yale University Press.

Petersen, Trond. 2004. Aage Røttger Sørebsen's Contributions to Quantitative Sociology from Studying Processes to Studying Structure. *Research in Social Stratification* 21: 27–44.

Piketty, Thomas. 2014. *Capital in the Twenty-First Century*. Cambridge: Harvard University Press.

Polanyi, Karl. 1957. The Economy as an Instituted Process. In *Trade and Market in Early Empires*, ed. Karl Polanyi, Conrad Arendberg, and Harry W. Pearson, 243–270. New York: Free Press.

Ricardo, David. [1817] 2004. *Principles of Political Economy and Taxation*. Mineola, NY: Dover.

Roemer, John. 1982. *A General Theory of Exploitation and Class*. Cambridge, MA: Harvard University Press.

Roth, Guenther. 1978. Footnote #67 to Volume 1, Chapter II, p. 211 in Max Weber. In *Economy and Society*. Berkeley: University of California Press.
Sen, Amartya. 1990. More Than 100 Million Women Are Missing. *The New York Review of Books*, 37 (20): 61–66.
Sen, Amartya. 1992. Missing Women. *British Medical Journal* 304: 586–587.
Smith, Adam. [1776] 1976. *The Wealth of Nations*. Chicago: The University of Chicago Press.
Solow, Robert. 2014. Thomas Piketty Is Right. *New Republic*, 22 April.
Sorensen, Aage B. 2000. Toward a Sounder Basis for Class Analysis. *American Journal of Sociology* 6: 1523–1558.
Stiglitz, J. 1977. The Theory of Local Public Goods. In *The Economics of Public Goods*, ed. M.S. Feldstein and R.P. Inman, 274–333. London: Macmillan.
Stiglitz, Joseph. 2012. *The Price of Inequality*. New York: W. W. Norton.
Stiglitz, Joseph. 2015a. New Theoretical Perspectives on the Distribution of Income and Wealth Among Individuals, Parts I–IV. NBER Working Paper Series, 21189, 21190, 21191, 21192.
Stiglitz, Joseph. 2015b. The Origins of Inequality, and Policies to Contain It. *National Tax Journal* 68 (2): 425–448.
Weber, Max. [1921] 1978. *Economy and Society*. Berkeley, CA: University of California Press.
Wright, Erik Olin. 1985. *Classes*. London: New Left Books.

CHAPTER 3

Thirteen Types of Rent in the Globalized World

Abstract Scarcity rent was already identified and analyzed by Ricardo, but the concept of solidarity rent is the present authors' innovation; then further sub-categories are introduced in this chapter. The rent-based interpretation of the importance of the natural resource sector is further generalized in this chapter. As Nicholas Kaldor and János Kornai have contended for decades, perfect competition exists only in economic textbooks. In reality, markets are oligopolistic not only in agriculture, in the extracting industries (as Ricardo thought), but also in the manufacturing and service sectors, too. The most efficient firms have always harness higher than average profits through larger mark-ups, or using this book's own terminology: they collect scarcity rent.

Keywords Scarcity rent · Solidarity rent · Oligopolies · Intellectual property rights · Occupational licenses · Minimum wages · Pay-as-you-go pensions · Trade unions

We believe that it is justified to make a distinction between two fundamentally different forms of rents: **scarcity rent** and **solidarity rent**. Scarcity rent was already identified and analyzed by Ricardo, but the concept of solidarity rent is our innovation; further sub-categories will be introduced later in this chapter. In Stiglitz (2015a) these two concepts are treated under a single heading: exploitation rent. In our view, this is grossly misleading.

P. Mihályi and I. Szelényi,
Rent-Seekers, Profits, Wages and Inequality,
https://doi.org/10.1007/978-3-030-03846-5_3

The best example of solidarity rent is the way *trade unions* work. Membership in a trade union reduces wage differentials. While nationwide unions tend to fight for the highest level of employment, branch-based unions fight for the highest possible wages for workers in their branch (and union). Especially, branch unions can push wages in their branch above market wages, hence secure rent to "members". Through the highly sophisticated institution of collective bargaining, unions prevent the use of wage incentives to pay more to the best workers, teachers or doctors at the advantage of those who underperform. This is particularly true in the public sector. Arguably, the income of those whose jobs are protected by unions or professional associations is composed of two factors: wages/salaries and rents. In developed liberal societies, one of the main functions of such institutions is to create conditions for solidarity. When the power of trade unions was on the rise, solidarity rent helped to reduce inequalities. However, in the context of the globalized world economy their weight declined during the last 30 years,[1] and this in turn was likely to have contributed to the stagnation of real wages for low-skilled manual workers in the manufacturing sectors of many advanced economies, and the United States in particular. The decline of the manufacturing sector, new forms of work and population aging were also playing a role in all this.

State-enforced *minimum wages* continue to exist in almost all developed countries since the first experiment introduced in Australia in 1896. There is no doubt; this is also a form of solidarity rent with the explicit aim of reducing income inequality. Today, among the 28 EU member states, 22 have such an institution. This list includes already Germany, where the introduction of the national statutory minimum wage occurred only in 2015. The parameters of the minimum-wage legislation in the United States are set by the federal labor

[1]On average across OECD countries, 30% of workers were members of a union in 1985. The corresponding figure in 2016 was only 17%. Today, union members tend to be predominantly male, middle-aged (between 25 and 54 years old), working with medium or high skills in medium or large firms, and on a permanent contract [http://www.oecd.org/els/emp/Flyer-Collective%20bargaining.pdf]. This decline was uniform across all member countries, with the notable exception of the Scandinavian countries and Iceland. Interestingly, the decline in union membership in the US has been rather small since the onset of the 2008 economic crisis, chiefly because the level was already low in 2006 already (11.5%) [https://stats.oecd.org/Index.aspx?DataSetCode=TUD]. The OECD websites were accessed on 5 August 2018.

law and a range of state and local laws. Employers have to pay workers the highest minimum wage prescribed by federal, state, and local law—irrespective of their workers' individual productivity measured at the workplace. As of January 2018, there were 29 states with a minimum wage higher than the federal minimum.[2] It is worth noting that solidarity rent often implies free riding as well, when even those who didn't bother to join a formal trade union (and pay union membership fees) benefit from the class struggle effort of the unionized workers in the form of higher wages or other entitlements. In so-called *closed shop* arrangements the employer agrees to hire—and retain in employment—only persons who are members in good standing of the representative trade union(s) of the given industry. In the United Kingdom and, to a lesser extent, in all other industrial nations, a closed-shop provision is seldom found in a written contract, but it was understood for decades that union members will walk off the job before they will work alongside non-unionists. This was commonly assumed among printers, dockworkers, and miners. Closed shops were declared illegal in the United States under the Taft-Hartley Act of 1947, but they continue to exist in practice.

Those who collect *pension in a pay-as-you-go system* also receive solidarity rent,[3] people who are on social welfare, whose health insurance is paid by taxpayers contributions do the same (as distinct from those who are in a funded private pension scheme, or whose healthcare benefits are paid from private insurance policies). Ideally, fiscal transfers always work as mechanisms of solidarity rent—a transfer from the rich to the poor. *Positive discrimination* (also known as affirmative action, positive action, or quota system in some countries) is a policy of protecting members of groups that are known to have previously suffered from discrimination (racial, ethnic, gender or politically defined). Such examples are to be found in all continents, including Europe.[4] For example in 2012, the European Union approved a plan for women to constitute

[2] https://en.wikipedia.org/wiki/Minimum_wage_in_the_United_States.

[3] It is noteworthy that in The World Top Income Database, the database underlying Piketty's book, such pensions are not taken into account, although in many countries such pensions constitute the bulk or at least a significant part of incomes flowing to the elderly population.

[4] Wikipedia lists 18 country examples, https://en.wikipedia.org/wiki/Affirmative_action, accessed on 24 April 2018.

40% of non-executive board directorships in large listed companies by 2020. The benefits of such policies—even if they are relatively small in the given country-context—all belong to our newly introduced category, the solidarity rent. They seek to achieve goals such as bridging inequalities in employment and pay, increasing access to education, promoting diversity, and redressing apparent past wrongs, harms, or hindrances.

Interestingly, even **under socialism** workers collected a rent on top of their wages: they had *almost absolute job security*. It was very difficult to lay off workers, even those who chronically underperformed, even if they showed up at work drunk. Hence, their income was only partially remuneration for their work, some of the income they collected almost as "owners" of the collective firm. Moreover, in the early decades of the Soviet-type system in Eastern Europe, young people of working-class descent were supported by positive discrimination, if they wanted to enroll university or become professional athletes competing at international level. Often, the combination of work/sports and university attendance was also encouraged, which in practice meant that these young workers were allowed to be absent from work without a commensurate reduction of their monthly pay.

Aage Sorensen (2000), whom we have already referred to, offered such a broad interpretation of rent: "Rents are payments to assets that exceed the competitive price or the price sufficient to cover costs and therefore exceeding what is sufficient to bring about the employment of the asset. (…) The existence of rent depends on the ability of the owner of the asset to control the supply".[5] Sorensen also pointed out that the association of rents with land is not required: "Rent will emerge on all productive assets that are in fixed supply and that actors need to maximize their wealth."[6] If we accept this framework, it follows that ownership of potentially rent-producing assets, such as licenses, credentials, access to loans to start new businesses or be self-employed is not restricted to wealthy capitalists. This is not a small social group. In 2016, the share of **self-employed** in the working population was 15.8% in the EU28 and 6.4% in the United States.[7] This is a particularly diverse group. At the top end are independent consultants with six-figure

[5]Op. cit., p. 1536.

[6]Op. cit., p. 1537.

[7]https://data.oecd.org/emp/self-employment-rate.htm, accessed on 13 January, 2018. For the possible complications arising from this, see Guerriero (2012) paper.

salaries; at the bottom are cleaners and security men on the minimum wage contracted by a company or an agency. This kaleidoscopic picture is further complicated by growing importance of the gig-economy, where people trying to top up their regular wage-type incomes are connected to their clients via websites (e.g. programmers, Uber-drivers or owners of rentable Airbnb apartments).

1 The Definition and the Main Types of Rent

We define rent in three different ways, but we mean the same thing in the three definitions and build them on a common economic base. In line with the Ricardian tradition, our approach is cost-based: observed transaction prices and incomes are compared with production costs or prices paid in an earlier transaction (e.g. selling a real estate × years after its purchase). The concept of diminishing subjective utility—the fact that consumers sometimes are willing to buy a single unit of the goods at a price higher than the equilibrium price and producers are willing to supply the first unit at a price lower than the equilibrium price—is not taken into account in our definition. In other words, our definition of rent is different from the textbook microeconomic concept of consumer surplus and producer surplus. We don't deny their existence, but we do not call them rents.

Following the line of thinking of Sorensen, we define the *sociological concept* of rent as the difference between what income would have been in "open relationship" by "closing" such relationships to certain individuals or categories of individuals. In simple algebraic form:

Income from closed relationship – income from open relationship – Rent

The *economic concept* of rent, as it was first developed by Ricardo for agricultural land and mines, could be easily generalized. Stiglitz (1992)—for example—built his definition on the observation that unlike in the case of most of the reproducible goods, higher payments for a certain type of assets or services will not elicit a greater supply.[8] Even if landlords received higher payments from peasants, the same amount of land would be available. The short-term supply of agricultural land

[8] Op. cit., pp. 357–359.

is inelastic with respect to rental price.[9] The same holds for athletes or celebrity performing artists: they cannot schedule more events, even if the spectators would be willing to pay twice as much for tickets as they do now. A similar mechanism works on certain good markets, say the market of widgets. Let us consider a market, where all firms except one, which is more efficient, have the same average cost in the production of widgets. Using his special position, this superefficient company would enjoy what an accountant might call profit, but economists would call "economic profit" *plus* rent. What this company receives in excess of what is required to induce the firm to enter the market is the rent.

$$(\text{Revenues} - \text{Expenditures}) - \text{economic profits}\ (\Pi) = \text{Rent}$$

In the world of standard textbook economics, sooner or later competition drives profits (Π) to zero. Then, if the difference between a firm's revenues and expenditures is still a positive value, that is the rent what we are looking for. It may be difficult to measure empirically all types of rents, but their existence can be demonstrated through counterfactual reasoning, using the first definition. What would have been the income of a closed group, if its members had competed in open relationships?

The *financial concept* of rent is routinely used to evaluate the successfulness of listed companies. One way to tell this is to look at the return on equity (ROE), a financial metric that measures the amount of net income returned as a percentage of shareholders equity. In business parlance, the term "excess profit" is used, but it is identical with our concept of rent. In many studies, this yardstick is 10%, the approximate maximum that is possible in an industry, where a minimum level of competition exists. Aswath Damodaran's data bank specialized on collecting ROE data for American listed companies, show that in 2017, a very good year for big business, the average ROE of 7300 US companies was about 14%—i.e. above the 10% yardstick.[10] Unsurprisingly, there is no direct correlation between the intensity of competition (i.e. the number of listed firms within a particular industry) and the absolute magnitude of ROE. In the given year, there were 18 firms in the Auto & Truck industry and 62 in the Auto Parts business. Nevertheless, ROE of

[9]As we argued already in Chapter 1 (p. 1), the long-term world history justifies the opposite conclusion.

[10]http://people.stern.nyu.edu/adamodar/New_Home_Page/datafile/roe.html, downloaded on 29 March 2018.

the former sector was 8.6%, while in the second one the calculated average was 24.1%. Wherever the products or the services are too complex for customers to understand, and where subsidies and complex regulations make the picture even more complicated, even bigger rents can be achieved (e.g. in healthcare services).

As we mentioned already, rent-seeking is often seen as *corruption.*[11] Whether a practice is corrupt or not is a matter of social judicial judgment. (This is the way Transparency International measures corruption: it is a judgment by experts.) An illegal economic transaction, which serves the interest of the public decision-maker, is the cleanest case of corruption. It is illegal for me to pay cash to a state official to exclude my competitors from bidding in a privatization or public procurement transaction, and if I do this, I can be charged for criminal activity. Liberal states with solid "legal rational authority", rule of law, laws which can be passed by legislatures and never retroactively, offer a clear criterion of legal corruption. In illiberal regimes, like Russia, China etc. the executive has excessive power and can change laws even retroactively and therefore *post facto* legalize otherwise "corrupt" activities.

Historically, the picture is more complicated. As Jens Ivo Engels (2014) argued in a superb monograph on the history of corruption from the early modern period to the twentieth century, protectionism and buying of state offices belonged to the normal toolkit of micropolitics, where favors were exchanged for favors. In the absence of competitive institutions in many countries kings had no other means to fill administrative positions (e.g. ministerial positions in the court, tax collection in the provinces), but simply relying on family relations, intuition or prepayment of some form. In the Catholic doctrines, the relationship of saints and worshippers worked in a similar way. The faithful asked the saints to intervene on their personal behalf with the almighty God and gave donations to confirm their sincerity. Thus, patronage and clientelism were for long centuries identical with good governance and virtuous morals. It was a gradual process, starting from the nineteenth century when the citizenry started to believe that political actions can be legitimized only by noble ideas, and therefore politics should be separated from personal interests to the maximum extent.

* * *

[11] See e.g. a broad collection of papers devoted to rent-seeking in the English language journal of the German *CESIfo DICE Report*, Vol. 13. No. 3. Autumn 2015.

Within a well-defined historical-political epoch—say lasting 20–30 years in which average people can make personal comparisons—rents can be **temporary** or **enduring**. An entrepreneur who invents new technology may collect rent for a while, but eventually his competitor will invest into the same or a similar technology and this rent will disappear, the incomes of competing entrepreneurs will be set by the supply and demand mechanism. There are many spectacular examples of this: the success of the Windows operating system invented by Microsoft, the rise of the cell phones which crushed the privileged position of copper-cable based telephone companies, or the shale revolution over the past decade which entirely reshaped the OPEC controlled traditional oil industry. Eastman Kodak Company, once a billion dollar company holding a dominant position in photographic film-making during most of the twentieth century, was forced to file for Chapter 11 bankruptcy protection in 2012.

Following Sorensen (1966, 2000) and also Marshall (1920), we can identify several enduring sources of rent. Some of the monopoly rents enjoyed by entrepreneurs are created *naturally*, since the costs of entering production within a given country are often prohibitive due to the increasing returns to scale (e.g. network industries). Rents may be created by governments, by issuing *concessions* to open mines or *licenses* to run tobacco and liquor shops.[12] Then, there are *personal* rents on biological endowments—for example special talent in popular sports or in arts at the level of individuals.[13] People with special endowments necessarily exist in all societies, and it makes sense to call a part of their above average incomes as rents (if they have). It is certainly more intuitive for us to speak of "rents" in this case, rather than "socialist exploitation", as Roemer (1982) labeled this phenomenon in the then existing socialist countries.[14]

[12] In the context of globalization, however, there is a growing number of companies worldwide in every industry, thus competition is actually increasing at the international level, even if national governments try to protect the "national champions".

[13] While it may be "politically incorrect", we do not reject—short of alternative empirical evidence—the possibility that genetic disposition also can be the source of rents. There is no genetic evidence that such rents exist, but a great deal of empirical observations suggests that they may. See e.g. Clark (2014).

[14] Op. cit., pp. 240–243. Roemer's main point was, of course, that to a certain extent income inequalities must exist even in an ideal (utopian) socialist society. The term "rent" is not even listed in the Index of Roemer's book, entitled *A General Theory of Exploitation and Class*.

Finally, there are extraordinary cases of ***resource endowments*** at the level of firms and countries exploiting mineral wealth and other types of geographical advantages such as access to open sea, sunny beaches or snowy mountains, etc. The rent-based interpretation of the importance of the **natural resource sector** can be further generalized. As Nicholas Kaldor (1934a, b, 1935, 1938) and János Kornai (1971) have contended for decades, perfect competition exists only in economic textbooks. In reality, markets are oligopolistic not only in agriculture, in the extracting industries, but also in the manufacturing and service sectors, too. The most efficient firms have always harness higher than average profits through larger mark-ups, or using our own terminology: they collect scarcity rent. While this interpretation of the ways markets work was and still is a minority proposition in the vast sea of the mainstream (neoclassical) economics, the following assertion is the bread-and-butter of the management science literature: **many important industries never have more than three significant competitors.**[15] The same trend in the literature also claims that in many markets the shares of the three leading companies reach a ratio of approximately 4:2:1—i.e. there is a significant market share difference even among the top firms. Data from US Census Bureau also support this claim. For example in 2012, the top four US firms' average share of total revenue on a sector-by-sector basis was close to 50% in IT, telecoms and media sector, 40% in retail trade and almost 40% in the finance and insurance sector.[16]

One explanation of the oligopolistic market structure is that large, multi-national firms have the means to negotiate special tax-deals with some governments—many of them enjoying an offshore status—through which they can increase their profits spectacularly (McDonalds, FIAT, Amazon, Apple, etc.). But there are further evidences. In an empirical OECD study—Andrews et al. (2015), a thorough econometric analysis showed that those 3400 firms that are the most productive are also

[15] This finding was first demonstrated by the founder of the Boston Consulting Group, Bruce Henderson (1976) and then later re-confirmed empirically on a much larger data set by Reeves et al. (2012). Since then, successful companies, like General Motors and others live according to this maxim. If they cannot become Number One or Two in an industry, they get out from that market and reinvest their resources somewhere else. [37]See *The Economist*, 26 March 2016.

[16] *The Economist*, 26 March 2016.

- larger,
- younger,
- own more patents,

than the rest and—most importantly from the perspective of the present paper—are usually

- part of a multi-national assemblage.[17]

In many businesses, the giant oligopolies do not cause much harm to consumers through higher-than-necessary prices, simply because for most consumers the services are free of charge. Google and Facebook are the most salient examples. These firms do generate monopoly rents because of their market dominance, but it is politically and morally difficult to punish them with anti-trust measures as long as the consumers do not feel themselves being hurt.[18] In such cases, rents are enjoyed by consumers even if markets are entirely open, but the objective of business is to increase the number of participants for maximizing the network effects. The important mechanism working here was recently identified by the 2014 Nobel Prize winner, Jean Tirole—the example of the so-called *two-sided markets.* Internet service providers like Google or Facebook, offer free services, provided the consumers are willing to accept the messages of advertisers. In this business model, the costs of the service, which is highly valuable for the non-paying consumers are actually levied on the merchants and the advertisers. Given the extraordinary importance of the IT-related consumption in the life of twenty-first-century households, this business model undoubtedly has an inequality-reducing impact.

According to the already quoted OECD study, the measured productivity differences are astonishingly high in cross-country comparisons. In terms of labor productivity, the best 100 firms in a given industrial sector, representing the global, worldwide technological frontier of that

[17]This research used the OECD-ORBIS firm-level productivity database of 300 thousand (!) companies pertaining to 23 OECD countries over the period 2001–2009. The industry details are at the 2-digit NACE level and comprise the nonfarm, non-financial business sector.

[18]As the 2014 Nobel Prize winner, Jean Tirole the nature of the so-called two-sided markets.

particular industry are 15 time more productive than the rest of the firms in the sample. Rivalry and selection at the global frontier are harsh nevertheless. Only 55% of the firms manage to remain at the global frontier from one year to the next, and after 5 years, less than 20% of firms are still there.[19]

A US study (Furman and Orszag 2015) has found that the top 10% of firms by profit have pulled away sharply from the rest. Their return on capital invested rose from more than 3 times that of the median firm in the 1990s to eight times. This is—as the quoted study suggests—way above any plausible cost of capital and likely to be pure rent. This increasingly skewed distribution of reported profits (containing rents) could explain certain type of wage inequalities as well. When an industry includes only a few big companies, they don't have to compete with one another as hard to attract employees—and so can end up paying their workers less than they would if there were true competition (labor market monopsony). However, the opposite mechanism may work as well. Because of the rent-component hidden in these firms' profitability, they can afford paying *all* or *some* of their employees above the industrial average. Indeed, one study showed that the size of wage differentials between American lower-level managers and low-tech, unskilled workers is associated with variations in pay between companies, not within them. In this case, wage inequalities are higher than suggested by a perfect competition model, not because the low-skilled workers underpaid, but because the qualified employees (i.e. the managers) are overpaid.[20] Using the terminology of another recent US study, we have strong reasons to speak of superstar wages in *superstar firms*.[21] Labor's falling share in economic output, which is one of the main drivers of Piketty's entire argumentation, is caused by the growing market share of superstar firms, rather than a general fall in labor share across all American firms.

Usually there are two interrelated factors behind this: (i) pioneering technology (a temporary advantage, as we argued earlier) and (ii) the economy of scale arising from the geographical concentration of firms within any given country. Both of these factors play a crucial role in generating revolutionary (or Schumpeterian) innovation. This line of

[19]Op. cit., p. 11.

[20]Quoted in *The Economist*, 1 October 2016.

[21]Autor et al. (2017).

argumentation is not entirely new either—their importance was already recognized by Alfred Marshall (1920).[22]

A lot of research has been focused recently on the role of the financial sector in increasing inequality. According to Stiglitz (2015b), the US financial sector grew before the 2008 crisis from 2 to 8% of GDP and profits grew to absorbing 40% of all corporate profits. Though there was a considerable increase in the amount of wealth to be managed (originating from oil-rich countries, Russia, China, etc.), Stiglitz is probably right to claim that the increase in the wealth-income ratio was not so substantial to account for the increase in the share of the financial sector. Nor can that sector's remuneration be accounted for by the improvements in their management of the funds, and even less so, by any improvement in overall economic performance. Our rent-based approach appears to be useful in elucidating the reported high profitability of such businesses. Quite certainly, one explanation of the monopoly rents is the oligopolistic concentration of the sector. Already in 2012, the top four American financial institutions earned close to 40% of the sector's total revenue.

It also seems plausible to accept as true that banks, insurance companies, hedge funds and brokerage firms in the Western world's capitals are receiving monopoly rents, based on their enduring experience, their brand names, the English language and—most importantly—the stability of the political and legal system built by two-three hundred years of history of liberal democracies. Given this historical heritage, it makes good sense for investors from all over the world to buy services from London or New York, even if these financial service prices contain a large element of rents.

There is no need to list examples to show that the term rent is used with different meaning not only in common parlance, but also in the scholarly literature. Now we try to delineate the various types of rents and their characteristics. In the spirit of Ricardo, Weber and Sorensen, we consider all incomes as rents, if they stem from ownership of *any* assets, where access to such assets is closed for other economic actors. Our list at present comprises of two major forms of rents and 13 sub-categories. Depending on the institutional setup of different countries, additional categories could be included[23] (Table 1).

[22]Op. cit., p. 268.

[23]See also Weeden and Grusky (2014, p. 476). Our typology is more elaborate, but similar.

Table 1 Different types of rents in the advanced economies

A	*Scarcity rents*	*Examples*
1	Ricardian rents	Agricultural land and mines
	Natural monopolies based on...	
2	—increasing returns and/or network effect	Airlines, internet, mobile telephones, etc.
3	—locational monopoly	Residential property, office buildings, hotels, etc.
4	Innovations in business	Facebook, google, etc.
5	Individual (genetic) endowments	Sports and arts
6	Competitive training	Sports
7	Social capital inherited from parents	Entrance to Ivy League universities
	Market limitations through	
8	—limiting the entry to the market by incumbents	Occupational licensing, cartels, lobbying and corrupt practices
9	—state induced monopolies	Innovations and new products (e.g. drugs) protected by intellectual property rights
B	*Solidarity rents generated by*	
10	—nation states	Trade protection, immigration control and positive discrimination
11	—collective bargaining	Local and national trade unions
12	—state induced welfare entitlements	Healthcare and pensions provided by the social security system
13	—charitable institutions	Aid and other forms of assistance provided within a country or internationally

Given the logic of Keynesian fiscal demand management, it is well understood since the Great Depression of 1929–1933 that all kinds of rents can be economically beneficial as long as they maintain or even boost consumption. This was a strong argument for unemployment benefits, but even conspicuous consumption can increase demand, create higher profits and wages, and hence indirectly contribute to wealth generation for the entire populace. At the same note, however, the international financial crisis starting in 2008 showed that **anti-crisis monetary policies** aiming to maintain the value of financial investments (primarily stocks and bonds) through *quantitative easing* were also beneficial for everybody from a stability point of view, but these measures **were intrinsically pro-rich**, since the rich own the bulk of such financial assets.

It is very important to underline that state-created monopolies, oligopolies or other forms of limiting labor market competition are not necessarily evil, as they are often justified by other social objectives rather than social equity. There are good and widely accepted reasons why **intellectual property** *rights* of pharmaceutical companies, individual innovators and artists are defended by "closure" in the Weberian sense through patents and copyrights.[24] It is not surprising that Aghion et al. (2015) found positive and significant correlations between innovativeness in the United States on the one hand, and top 1% income shares on the other. Similarly, it makes a great deal of sense to require state permission for firms to build nuclear power stations, or even simple two storey family houses. Few economists would criticize the state-enforced prohibitions of child labor—both at the national and the international level—even if the implication is that certain goods or services become more expensive than under unlimited wage competition.[25]

It is in the general interest that physicians have to acquire a special **occupational license** (e.g. a university diploma) before they can start treating sick people. But in other cases, the evidence to justify such a limitation of competition is not straightforward at all, and it is *a fortiori* more dubious for the broadening of such practices. According to one study, in 1950 one in twenty employed Americans required a license to work. By 2017 that had risen to more than one in five. About 1100 occupations are regulated in at least US state, but fewer than 60 are regulated in all 50. Bartenders must have licenses in 13 states; manicurists are licensed everywhere but Connecticut. Louisiana licenses florists. In other words, the erection of such labor market barriers is largely ad hoc in many states reflecting local lobby power of the suppliers of particular type of services more than anything intrinsic, explicable argumentation.[26] In short, there is a lot of bad rent here.

The deregulation wave of the 1980s under Mrs. Thatcher and Mr. Reagan had an important bias. As a recent Bagehot-essay in *The Economist* wisely noted some of the working class closed shops, such as printers and air traffic controllers were broken, but professional close

[24] Having stated this as our conclusion, we are of fully aware of the opinion of others—e.g. Lindsey and Teles (2017)—who marshalled strong arguments against the current level of state protection of intellectual property rights.

[25] According to the ILO (2017), child labor is concentrated primarily in agriculture (71%), 17% in services; and 12% in the industrial sector, including mining. In other words, child labor is essentially a pre-capitalist heritage of the modern world.

[26] *The Economist*, 17 February 2014.

shops in the world of academia—i.e. among the highly educated, highly placed, high-income earners—remained rife with restrictive practices (e.g. the system of tenure). Academic publishers combine several sorts of rent-seeking together. They get free content, free peer-reviews and a lot of editorial work, because university faculty is under heavy pressure to publish and co-operate with the journals. These journals have a guaranteed market, as well, since university libraries cannot discontinue the subscription of the established academic journals.[27]

In sum, we do not reject the "visible hand" as a matter of principle. If the state interferes in the labor market in order to create "fair" competition, this is certainly desirable, precisely because it reduces rent-seeking (e.g. the exploitation of unprotected children). Other types of regulations and interventions of the visible hand (e.g. land use by-laws in urban areas) are more problematic and they could be assessed—i.e. justified or condemned—if at all, on a case-by-case basis only.

2 Institutional Consequences of Rents

In this book, we have stated already that if the rise of rents begins to match or even overtake the growth of incomes from profits and wages, this can have major (often unintended and undesired) institutional consequences. We can think of at least two such institutional consequences. Firstly, certain type and some level of rent are necessary for social cohesion and innovation in society. Such rents may be seen as "deserved", but at one level, they are still "unearned". The major legitimacy claim of market capitalism is meritocracy. At one point, however, rents generated by any means can be seen as "excessive", if public opinion judges it of too much for those who "did not work for it".

Most people accept some rent to drug manufacturers/innovators, but there may be a ceiling of how much is seen as "reasonable" and how much is judged as "exploitive". The same goes for social benefits. In civilized societies most people accept that the poor (or disabled) should have some social support—even if it is "unearned"—but at one point it may be judged to be "far too much". Even in the United States, the most sacred social institution like Social Security has been challenged, but so far unsuccessfully. Should Social Security be "privatized", hence turned

[27] *The Economist*, 24 March 2018.

it from "rent collection" to "profit incomes" on deposits made during lifetime? This is an often discussed alternative to the present arrangement, although given the broad political support for Social Security it is likely to remain the sacred cow of US politics (which actually works quite well and there is no reasonable proposal to replace it with a market-based alternative).

Secondly, if the wealth of individuals comes increasingly from rent rather than wages or profits, there is little institutional incentive that rent will be reinvested in the most efficient way. The *nouveau riche* or the inheritors are tempted to waste the rent they collected: Easy come, easy go. Profit maximizing entrepreneurs tend to invest their profits in optimal ways to fight off competitors. Rent collectors don't face competition; rent can be spent as "conspicuous consumption". The *nouveau riche* entrepreneur tends to use a chauffeur-driven Mercedes, or private plane well before they can afford it. The second and especially third generation "inheritors" may spend their inheritance in a good case on charity, in a bad case on conspicuous consumption. Thomas Mann's novel, *The Buddenbrook House* tells such a story. While the first generation accumulates, the second generation sustains, the third generation tends to waste the remaining family wealth. The absence of an institutional mechanism for owners of wealth to use it the most efficient way can have devastating social and economic consequences. It can lead to state failure and economic stagnation or even collapse.

3 Measuring Capital and Wealth

Measuring the stock of capital (K) is fraught with theoretical contradictions. Relatively to this, it is easy to measure wealth at aggregate (national) level. The fundamental critique of the neo-classical capital theory goes back to the writings of P. Sraffa, J. Robinson, and N. Kaldor in the 1950s and early 1960s. This debate is known in textbooks of the history of economic thoughts as "Cambridge Capital Controversy"—an allusion to the affiliation of the main protagonists of the debate in Cambridge (USA) and Cambridge (UK).[28]

As the UK Cambridge people convincingly argued, capital—together with profit and rent—are rather heuristic classifications. In fact, it is very

[28] For more recent broader discussion of the consequences see e.g. Keen (2011), Felipe and McCombie (2013), and Moseley (2014).

difficult to find statistical measures for any of these concepts. Even if such headings are listed among the measured economic variables, they often reflect merely the country's prevailing taxation framework, rather than the underlying political economic reality. For example, in both advanced and less advanced market economies, there are strong incentives to declare labor income (wages) as capital income (profits). In the Anglo-Saxon countries, the main motive to buy real estate for housing purposes rather than renting a place to live is explained by the deductibility of interest expenditures from personal income tax. The incentives of the self-employed, already mentioned at the beginning of this chapter, are largely a matter of taxation rules. Hence, when the rich or the relatively rich are paying low taxes, it is hard to know whether the system of taxation is not sufficiently progressive or the crux of the problem is tax avoidance and tax evasion. It is not by chance that The World Bank decided to measure inequality by consumption rather than income.

Aggregate wealth is easily captured both in conceptual and statistical data collection terms. In contrast, *private* wealth, which is in the focus of Piketty's theory,[29] available only from tax records which are incomplete or unreliable for the very rich everywhere, especially in post-socialist countries. It is not by chance that there is not a single post-communist country in the World Top Income Database with sufficiently long time coverage. Surveys are no solution either, as in medium and small countries there are few observations of the top 1.0 or the top 0.1% of the population.

Privately owned capital is composed of assets directly involved in economic production. K needs to produce profits in the long run as otherwise, banks will not provide funding and eventually the firm will be beaten by competition. In contrast, many forms of private wealth are not meant to generate a financial return. Real estate, works of art, pension entitlements, life, and health insurance policies or cash holdings are the trivial examples. Wealth can operate as or converted into K, but the opposite transformation is also important when inter-generational transfer takes place in the form of inheritance. When marriages are broken, for example, the divorce often implies conversions from K to wealth.

[29] In his interpretation, public wealth in the developed countries is insignificant, or even negative due to the accumulated public debt. Piketty (2014, p. 48.) We shall return to this issue above in a minute.

As Stiglitz (2015a) demonstrated in a book-size paper, much of wealth is generated not by profits, but through rents arising from deviations from the standard competitive paradigm.[30] His example states that firms can generate rents for their owners by creating and exploiting *information asymmetries.*[31] But, more importantly in our view, changes in wealth—both upwards and downwards—are also associated with *relative asset price fluctuations.* The values of real estate, works of arts, as well as the value of stocks and foreign currency holdings oscillate in broad ranges around the average rate of inflation.

In an attempt to measure K according to the logic of his two-class model, Piketty disregarded further specificities of the twenty-first-century advanced capitalism. In reality, the total value of physical assets owned by flesh and blood capitalists and used primarily for generating profits is relatively small. According to the NBER, privately owned non-residential assets (equipment and structures) amount to merely 32% of the total accumulated fixed assets of the US economy.[32] A considerably large part of K is publicly owned (transport infrastructure, health, educational and cultural facilities, military assets, etc.). The accumulation of these assets in the hands of the state from the taxes paid by households and businesses is not responsible for any harm to ordinary workers or employees, with the situation is usually the contrary. In many dimensions, the use of these assets by ordinary citizens is free of charge and hence constitutes a very important component of their living standards. In 2013, according to the estimates of NBER, the share of public ownership within the net stock of fixed assets (including consumer durables) was 25%. Beyond this, America's federal government owns 25% of the country's land.[33] Therefore disregarding state assets, as Piketty did, was greatly misleading.[34]

[30] Op. cit., Part I., p. 8.

[31] Op. cit., Part I., p. 26.

[32] Bureau of Economic Analysis, last revised on September 17, 2014. The value of land is not included in the NBER wealth account data cited here.

[33] *The Economist*, 13 June 2015.

[34] Op. cit., pp. 123–131.

References

Aghion, Philippe, Ufuk Akcigit, Antonin Bergeaud, Richard William Blundell, and David Hemous. 2015. Innovation and Top Income Inequality. CEPR Discussion Paper No. 10659.

Andrews, Dan, Chiara Criscuolo, and Peter N. Gal. 2015. Frontier Firms, Technology Diffusion and Public Policy: Micro Evidence from OECD Countries. The Future of Productivity: Main Background Papers. Paris: OECD.

Autor, David, David Dorn, F. Lawrence Katz, Christina Patterson, and John Van Reenen. 2017. The Fall of the Labor Share and the Rise of Superstar Firms. NBER Working Paper No. 23396, May.

Clark, G. 2014. *The Son Also Rises*. Princeton: Princeton University Press.

Engels, Jens Ivo. 2014. *Die Geschichte der Korruption: Von der Frühen Neuzeit bis ins 20. Jahrhundert* [The History of Corruption: From the Early Modern Period to the 20th Century]. Frankfurt am Main: Fischer.

Felipe, Jesus, and John S.L. McCombie. 2013. *The Aggregate Production Function and the Measurement of Technical Change: 'Not Even Wrong'*. Cheltenham: Edwar Elgar.

Furman, Jason, and Peter Orszag. 2015. A Firm-Level Perspective on the Role of Rents in the Rise in Inequality. Presentation at "A Just Society" Centennial Event in Honor of Joseph Stiglitz Columbia University, 16 October. Manuscript.

Guerriero, Marta. 2012. The Labor Share of Income Around the World: Evidence from a Panel Dataset. University of Manchester, Institute for Development Policy and Management, Working Paper No. 32.

Henderson, Bruce. 1976. The Rule of Three and Four, ld. https://www.bcgperspectives.com/content/Classics/strategy_the_rule_of_three_and_four/.

International Labour Office. 2017. *Global Estimates of Child Labour: Results and Trends, 2012–2016*. Geneva.

Kaldor, Nicholas. [1934a] 1960: A Classificatory Note on the Determinateness of Equilibrium. In *Essays on Value and Distribution*, 13–33. London: Duckworth.

Kaldor, Nicholas. [1934b] 1960. The Equilibrium of the Firm. In *Essays on Value and Distribution*, 34–50. London: Duckworth.

Kaldor, Nicholas. [1935] 1960. Market Imperfection and Excess Capacity. In *Essays on Value and Distribution*, 62–80. London: Duckworth.

Kaldor, Nicholas. [1938] 1960. Professor Chamberlin on Monopolistic and Imperfect Competition. In *Essays on Value and Distribution*, 81–95. London: Duckworth.

Keen, Steve. 2011. *Debunking Economics—Revised and Expanded Edition*. London and New York: Zed Books.

Kornai, János. 1971. *Anti-equilibrium (On Economic Systems: Theory and the Tasks of Research)*. Amsterdam: North-Holland Publishing.

Lindsey, Brink, and Steven M. Teles. 2017. *The Captured Economy (How the Powerful Enrich Themselves, Slow Down Growth and Increase Inequality)*. New York: Oxford University Press.

Marshall, Alfred. 1920. *Principles of Economics*, 8th ed. London: Macmillan.

Moseley, F. 2014. Piketty and Marginal Productivity Theory: A Superficial Application of a Very Bad Theory. Manuscript. https://www.aeaweb.org/conference/2015/retrieve.php?pdfid=942. Date last accessed 5 December 2016.

Piketty, Thomas. 2014. *Capital in the Twenty-First Century*. Cambridge: Harvard University Press.

Reeves, Martin, Mike Deimler, George Stalk, and Filippo L. Scognamiglio Pasini. 2012. BCG Classics Revisited, the Rule of Three and Four. www.bcgperspectives.com/content/articles/business_unit_strategy_the_rule_of_three_and_four_bcg_classics_revisited/.

Roemer, John. 1982. *A General Theory of Exploitation and Class*. Cambridge, MA: Harvard University Press.

Sorensen, Aage B. 1996. The Structural Basis of Inequality. *American Journal of Sociology* 101 (5): 1333–1365.

Sorensen, Aage B. 2000. Toward a Sounder Basis for Class Analysis. *American Journal of Sociology* 6: 1523–1558.

Stiglitz, Joseph. 1992. *Economics*. New York and London: W.W. Norton.

Stiglitz, Joseph. 2015a. New Theoretical Perspectives on the Distribution of Income and Wealth Among Individuals, Parts I–IV. NBER Working Paper Series, 21189, 21190, 21191, 21192.

Stiglitz, Joseph. 2015b. The Origins of Inequality, and Policies to Contain It. *National Tax Journal* 68 (2): 425–448.

Weeden, Kim A., and David Grusky. 2014. Inequality and Market Failure. *American Behavioral Scientist* 58 (3): 473–491.

CHAPTER 4

Class Reproduction of the Upper Middle Class (Top 20%)

Abstract The wealth of billionaires (the top 0.1%) is less of the authors' concern than the living standards of the "Joneses". People are likely to be more interested how the gap between them and people they know is increasing. It seems that entry/exit into and from the top 0.1% is relatively open. Many of the wealthiest people from the United States to China, Russia, or Central Europe come from humble background. But, can we detect a trend for the upper middle class (top 20%) to become increasingly closed? The answer is: yes. This chapter identifies three mechanisms of the increasing closure: elite education, inheritance of wealth (chiefly real estate) and assortative mating.

Keywords Wealth · Inheritance · Assortative mating · Elite education · Credentialing · Re-feudalization · Patrimonial capitalism · Illiberal state

Our second concern with **Piketty**'s argument is that he **over-emphasizes the income/wealth gain of the top 1.0%**. The ridiculous gains on the very top are obvious, but the question is how significant are they? The slogan "we are the 99%" for a while appeared to be a mobilizing force. Even social scientists paid particular attention to the income/wealth gain of the top 1 or top 0.1%.

There are two reasons why focusing on the top 1 and especially top 0.1% is misleading: First, the wealth of billionaires is less of concern than

P. Mihályi and I. Szelényi,
Rent-Seekers, Profits, Wages and Inequality,
https://doi.org/10.1007/978-3-030-03846-5_4

the living standards of the "Joneses". People are likely to be more interested how the gap between them and people they know is increasing (if it does). Second, we know relatively little about the composition on the very top of the income/wealth distribution. It is at least conceivable that entry/exit into and from the top 0.1% is relatively open. Many of the wealthiest people from the United States to China, Russia, or Central Europe come from humble background. Think of Bill Gates, George Soros, the Russian Boris Berezovsky, or Lőrinc Mészáros, the close friend of the Hungarian Prime Minister, Viktor Orbán. Hence, the liberal dream that positions at the top are open to all seems to have some empirical support. Our key hypothesis is (to be tested eventually by empirical research) that the gap between to top 20% of income/wealth distribution and the rest of the population is increasing. We call this "upper middle class" and we hypothesize that this class is increasingly based on inheritance and increasingly closed.

In the United States, the increasing gap between the top 5–20% and the bottom 10–20% is gaining a great deal of attention in recent literature. Several authors emphasize that the income/wealth share going to the top 5–20% has been increasing (though not as fast as the gains of the top 1%), while at the bottom 10–20% incomes stagnate or decline. At the very bottom, there is just no wealth accumulated (those born at the bottom of social hierarchy may inherit debt rather than wealth).

We seem to know more about processes under way at the bottom of society, hence about poverty, but the upper middle class for some reason did not capture the attention of social scientists. There is substantial literature on the "middle class", though the question of the growth of middle class usually is cast as a problem of "collective mobility", hence the reduction of differences between middle third, fourth, and fifth deciles. You have a middle class society as long as those in the middle tend to converge.[1]

In this book, our focus in contrast is the upper middle class. The question we pose—in absence of data and analysis mainly for future research—can we detect a trend for the upper middle class to become increasingly closed, or people in these structural positions increasingly functioning as a "privileged rank" rather than a "class"? On the top of

[1]For a recent good quality intellectual survey of the discussion on the importance of the middle class under the supervision of the International Labour Organization (ILO), see Vaughan-Whitehead (2016).

social hierarchy, we find "classes" as long as exit and entry from and into these positions is relatively open, based on merit and effort and less on inheritance.

Our first hypothesis—about the emergence of a "dominant rank" on the top of society—would be supported, if data would show that beyond the increasing share of incomes/wealth of the top 5–20% is also matched with decreasing upward and downward mobility within the same generation or cross-generations. Especially if the next generation becomes "inheritants", then their wealth is less and less dependent on their "merit" or "effort", but their source is rent as defined above. They are becoming a new "nobility" or even "aristocracy". To the best of our knowledge, such data are not available for post-communist countries, but according to the large body of recent literature there is indeed such a tendency in the United States.

This question was also raised by Piketty when he wrote about the emergence of "patrimonial capitalism", but he never clarified to what extent such increasing differences can be attributed to increasing gap between profits and wages or the increasing importance of rents. Guy Standing (2017), the prophet of guaranteed basic income raises this issue as well, even when it is in contradiction with his proposal to offer the same basic income when he claims that we are living in the second Gilded Age, where the increasing share of income goes to a small circle of rentiers. Piketty (2018) in a recent paper now also focuses on the top 10%. He shows that in advanced economies the share of incomes of the top 10% was high in 1900 (over 45% in Europe and Japan, just over 40% in the United States). In all of these countries income share of the top 10% bottomed out around 1970 (all these countries had between 30 to 34% of the share of all income), but by 2010 they already regained the ground lost during the mid-twentieth century. In the United States, the top 10% almost earned half of all incomes. Piketty also shows the rather dramatic drop of the income share of the bottom 50% from 20% in 1962 to 12% by 2014.

It can, of course, be debated whether it matters at all if wealth (privileged status) is inherited, hence comes from rent or comes from wages/profits. One possible argument is that irrespective whether wealth in inherited or acquired on competitive markets the owners of wealth will spend it on consumption (driving up demands and stimulating economic growth) or even invest it in creating new jobs. This is indeed possible, but in case of wealth stemming from rent, there is no social or economic mechanism, which forces the inheritors to invest the wealth inherited as rent to invest it in an economically efficient way. We analyzed before the theory of exploitation of Marx from volume I. of *The Capital*, where he claims that the capitalist is forced by the competition to invest his profits in an efficient way, otherwise he will be loose out in of business. No such mechanism operates in case of a feudal landlord who can spend the "surplus" he expropriates from his serves on conspicuous consumption—since his fellow landlord is likely to do the same.

In the recent US social science literature several authors—some political left-winger or liberals, others conservatives or right-wingers—report such a "rank" type of stratification of what used to be "upper middle class". For a left-leaning or liberal formulation of this proposition, see Robert D. Putnam "*Our Kids: The American Dream in Crisis*" (2015), and a similar analysis is offered from the conservative Richard V. Reeves in his "*Dream Hoarders: How the American Upper Middle Class Is Leaving Everyone Else in the Dust*" (2017). With some simplifications, both authors identify three mechanisms of the increasing "closure" of the "upper middle class":

- elite education,
- inheritance of wealth, and
- assortative mating.

1 Elite Education

a. In order to get admission to elite schools, like Ivy League Colleges it is a substantial advantage if one's parents are graduates from those colleges. This is called "legacy admission", where students get extra points for admission if parents are graduates from the college. George W. Bush was admitted to Yale not so much based on his high-school records or SAT, but because his father already graduated from Yale (and the younger Bush did not do all that well at Yale earning mainly B's and C's).[2] Elite universities usually do not release data on legacy admissions, but it is estimated that they may add up to the third of incoming classes. This effect is reinforced by

[2] Riviera (2015, p. 12).

the fact that students from expensive private high schools tend to do better in SAT exams. In such private high schools (where just the tuition may add up to $200,000, teachers are better paid, are of higher quality, fellow students are very competitive and teaching focuses on producing high GRE scores for their graduates.[3]

There is also a substantial body of social science literature, which shows, or at least claims in a credible way that how SAT or IQ is set up has a strong bias for upper middle class. It measures upper middle class "intelligence", with more emphasis on "cultural capital" or "theoretical knowledge" (to put it with Bourdieu), which is not higher level or more intelligence than what working of lower middle class kids have, just different.[4]

b. Graduation from elite schools is a significant advantage on the job market. Such graduates get better and more highly paid jobs. Elite firms (for instance law firms) tend to hire applicants, whose habitus is similar to those who sit on the recruitment committees.[5] Hence. upper middle class kids get to privileged colleges, which secure better jobs, with higher incomes for them, so the reproduction of upper middle class is secured. Putnam claims not only that this mechanism works, but its effect is getting stronger with time.[6]
c. There is an additional mechanism of closure in the educational system and that is **credentialing**. Education is often conceptualized in terms of human capital investment. It is usually assumed that human capital invested into education leads to productivity gains and higher incomes for the better educated result from this productivity gain. But especially powerful professional associations (such as American Medical Association, or American Law Boards) requiring bar examinations play a role to control the supply of occupations under their jurisdiction, hence they may drive up incomes for those occupations by adding a rent to their income from work.

[3] Khan (2011).
[4] Riviera, op. cit., p. 276.
[5] Riviera, op. cit., pp. 14–16.
[6] Op. cit., p. 187.

The emphasis on credentialing (rather just on education or training) may have consequences on what kind of knowledge will be required from candidates seeking valued credentials. Not all knowledge required to pass critical exams will have productivity gains, it may be just knowledge, which is useful to screen candidates for such credentials. This is what Bourdieu and Passeron ([1970] 1977) called "cultural capital" as distinct from "human capital". Cultural capital serves more the purposes of the reproduction of the "patrimonial upper middle class", rather than increasing the productivity of the graduate. For parents, it may cost as much as $300,000–400,000 just to get their children an Ivy League BA or BSc—but an Ivy League degree will elevate their the children to the status of "nobility". Employers will seek Ivy League graduate not necessarily since their technical skills are better, but because hiring such people will add to the prestige of their institution. Rivera (2015) even shows that among elite university graduates people from upper middle class background are more likely to get jobs in highly paid elite firms, even if the grade point average was the same, since those who administer recruiting are also usually upper middle class and their recruit on the basis of "habitus", the recruit people who are "just like themselves".[7]

2 Inheritance of Wealth

Inheritance of wealth is probably very high in the top 1–0.1%, but it is arguably substantial in the upper middle class as a whole. As we pointed already out, it is not obvious whether inherited wealth will operate as profit of rent. In principle, inherited wealth also can be invested in an efficient way, but the inheritor can behave as a feudal landlord hence spending his wealth on fun, creating on the short term increased consumer demand, but undermining in the long term the profitability of his business. Given the rising life expectancy in the advanced countries, most people inherit wealth from his/her own parents in a relative high age. This is not the time, when the newly acquired wealth is all used for future businesses.

In case of the upper middle class, **inheritance of real estate** (and pension savings) is especially important. According to Richard Reeves, 44% of the children of parents of the upper quintiles of wealth tend to end up

[7]Rivera (2015, pp. 12–13).

in the upper wealth quintile[8]; and only one-third of them will drop into the second or lower quintiles. Surpassingly, the social reproduction seems to be less rigid at the bottom social hierarchy. Only one-third of children who were born in the bottom quintile of wealth distribution will stay in the bottom quintile. Pablo Mitnik et al. (2015) surprisingly found that intergenerational elasticity is greater in the lowest quintiles than in the highest quintile.[9] This may be especially true for the United States, with a large immigrant population, who tend to start their American life in the lowest quintiles. The children of European, Chinese, Indian (and even Latino) parents tend to be upwardly mobile. It is likely that Mitnik and Grusky might have reached different conclusion if they studied African-Americans, who are not only overrepresented in the lowest quintiles, but their children are more likely to be stuck there. Due to the "underclass" formation mechanism, which tends to ethnicize poverty, the underprivileged class position of African/Americans may limit the upward mobility of ghetto African-American poor youth. Dalton Conley (1999) reported such a rigid "class reproduction" for poor African-Americans in his wonderful book, *Being Black and Being in the Red*. One important reason is the absence of wealth ownership by parents; hence Conley's policy recommendation was to offer compensation for slavery for African-Americans. According to Conley the real disadvantage of lower class African American is primarily not the wage/income, but the wealth gap.

This may stand also for the Roma in Central Europe today. Under socialism Roma were also discriminated against, but at least their rate of employment was high. Unemployment exploded in this population by the last years of socialism and after the regime change. It is generally accepted that up to half of this population is at the bottom of income/wealth hierarchy.

It is conceivable that the reproduction of the upper middle class as a privileged "estate" is primarily not driven by the accumulation of capital (that may stand more for the top 1–5%), but the inheritance of valuable real estates, houses, condos, and works of art. The increase of value of residential real estate—rent in the classical definition of Ricardo—was quite extraordinary in the last few decades in the United States, in most

[8] Reeves (2017, p. 63).

[9] Cited by Reeves (2017, p. 62).

European countries, including increasingly post-communist Central Europe (and also in Russia and China).

Such a gain in residential real estate value is exceptionally uneven. According to some data, in the United States over the past 3–4 decades, the increase of value of residential real estate nationwide was close to the increases of average incomes. This is, of course, inevitable; otherwise, it would be impossible for young, average income earners to enter the real estate market. Nevertheless, in some clusters of the real estate markets (certain areas of New York, especially Manhattan, Boston, San Francisco, and other highly desirable residential areas) the increase of value was breathtaking. Condos, for instance, brought on upper West side in New York in the mid-1960s for $200,000 may now be valued at $2 million. Hence, owners have a massive gain in rent. Location, location, location: this is the reviled wisdom in real estate business. Well-to-do people, who could afford to buy houses or condos in well-to-do areas multiplied their wealth and intriguingly even the 2008 global financial crisis and the collapse of real estate markets did not hit them as hard as the poor were hit. Even if they lost some assets, it was soon not only recovered but real estate values in elite areas are at all-time highs. The children or grandchildren of those who had the resources to invest into elite areas inherit now millions of dollars and have very different life chances from the children of middle class, working class and in particular the poor Blacks. The sub-prime mortgage crisis hit particularly hard the poorest of the poor. They not only lost their lifetime investments, but often their houses were put on foreclosure and some joined the ranks of the homeless.

Urbanization, the decline of agriculture and small townships previously surviving or doing even fairly well is likely to hit very hard by migration from these often isolated places to larger towns and cities which offer job opportunities. As younger people leave these smaller towns, the real estate market collapses, houses built just a few decades ago with great effort and investments have absolutely no value, there is just no demand for them. This is certainly true for post-communist Central Europe, where the collective farm system kept the population in agrarian villages. A rather extreme example is Hungary where during the 1960s and 1970s given the openness of Hungarian communist regime to the agrarian “second economy”, small agrarian producers did quite well, and then they invested their substantial second economy earnings in building new houses for themselves. With the destruction of the agrarian second economy, the economic base of these villages collapsed, population is declining and otherwise reasonable quality housing left empty, many up for sale, but no buyers.

Such functioning of the housing market results in a massive redistribution of wealth from lower and middle classes to the upper middle class and creates a boundary between the upper middle class (the new nobility) and the rest of the society (the struggling or even impoverished people dependent on market defined wages and incomes) what is increasingly difficult to cross.

3 Assortative Mating

The third mechanism of the reproduction and increased closure of the upper middle class—and the reproduction of the underclass—is assortative mating. People (or estate) tend to marry partners from the same class or estate. The difference in when women start establishing families cuts along many of the same lines that divide societies in other ways (e.g. geography, profession), but the biggest one is education. Women with college degrees have their first children many years later than those without—and often use the years in between to finish school and build their careers and incomes. In the United States, this difference is currently seven years.[10] The labor market explanation is simple: (i) a college degree is increasingly essential to earning a middle class wage; (ii) older parents have more years to earn money to invest in the future of their children. In the case of women without some kind of higher education, their pregnancies are more likely to be unintended, and they are more likely unmarried. These factors are all hardship factors from the perspective of their children both psychologically and financially.

But a further social gap exists even among college graduates. There is some credible evidence that graduates from **elite schools**—especially Ivy League—tend to marry partners who are graduates from similar (though not necessarily the same) institutions. According to Putnam, during the early twentieth century cross-class mating was far from uncommon, but by the end of the century the mating among partners with similar education increased substantially.[11] Schwarz and Mare (2005) supported such claim with careful quantitative analysis. *The Economist* in an article on

[10] "The Age That Women Have Babies: How a Gap Divides America", *The New York Times*, 9 August 2018.

[11] Putnam (2015, p. 40).

January 22, 2015 went as far as to claim the birth of "A new America aristocracy"—and not only in the United States, but elsewhere as well. Three successive cohort studies of 70 thousand children born in the UK in 1946, 1958, and 1970 showed that childhood circumstances determined by the social status of their parents profoundly influence the children's lifetime inequalities in spite of all the pro-poor welfare measures introduced by successive British governments.[12]

Assortative mating of elite school graduates makes it likely that both spouses are likely to get privileged jobs in a privileged institution—hence the income may include some rent over and above their market earned salary. So, given the increasing class homogeneity of elite school students, it is also likely that both spouses inherit substantial wealth as their grandparents pass away, this is the drawing the border between the upper middle class and the rest of the society even sharper and more difficult to cross. In the United States—and to some extent even in Western Europe—the question of assortative meeting was researched extensively.

We know relatively little about assortative mating during socialism and post-communism. Personal observations suggest that in the early epoch of state socialism—in Central Europe during the late 40s and most of the 50s cross-class mating was quite common, was even seen as "politically correct". From the 60s onward until the fall of communism here might have been a trend for professionals mating professionals, cadre kids marrying cadre kids (but we have no solid empirical evidence to support this). What has happened after the post-communist transformation? We can only make guesses. There is some evidence from China, Russia, and Central Europe that children of moneyed aristocracy and children of political aristocracy often intermarry. The new moneyed aristocracy receives political protection and special excess to markets, auctions controlled by the political class. The political bosses tend to hide their own private wealth (if they got any—whether they do it is only a guess by their political opponents), but now the enrichment of their son or daughter-in-law (or incidentally sisters, brothers, or parents) makes family enrichment a little more legitimate (or at least less vulnerable to legal challenges). We also do not know what kind of education the children of the new moneyed or political nobility get. But there is substantial difference in quality of education, private schools offer better training and

[12] Pearson (2016).

children of the "new nobility" is more likely to spend a year or two in good foreign schools as exchange students and more likely to eventually graduate from elite Western colleges, joining the privileges of West European and especially American upper middle class.

Our most important hypothesis is that even in that part of the world, the socially and economically most burning question is not so much the outrages enrichment of the top 1 or 0.1%, but the increasingly almost feudalv, estate-like separation of the upper middle class from the rest of the society. It is a challenging empirical task to find out exactly where this boundary is in the post-communist countries. Does the upper middle class or the "ruling estate" mean the top 5, 10, or 20%? This may vary from country to country and from time to time and it can only be established by careful empirical research. Just measuring inequality of incomes is only the first—and relatively speaking easiest task. One needs estimate wealth and inheritance of privileges in incomes, wealth, social networks and assortative mating.

We admire Bálint Magyar's powerful theory of the "mafia state" (discussed at greater in Chapter 5), but in our reading he narrows down the privileged, re-feudalized population too much. He may not appreciate enough that the political class while undoubtedly trying to enrich themselves and their family (and as we can see in the case of Donald Trump's presidency, not only in post-communist countries, but even in the United States) its only and main aim may not be just self-enrichment. The goal function of all politicians is to gain as much political power as they can and to stay in power as long as possible. This requires the building and maintenance of a large population of clients—some very well off, some just better off than they would be on competitive market. It is a big assumption that all those clients are "Strohmann", hence all that they do is that they hide as their personal wealth the wealth which actually belongs to the political bosses. Some of the clients live a luxurious lifestyle, or at least they have a better living that similarly qualified people who did not "plead loyalty" to the political bosses have had to struggle on competitive market (if they are seen as disloyal may even have to struggle on "uneven field").

As we emphasized several times earlier in this book, rent per se is not evil, it can even be beneficial in offering some stability in general and especially in the social order (like solidarity rent may do if not excessive). On occasions, even rent-seeking may be necessary. Our key point though is this: if Piketty is right—and he seems to be very much on track at least in post-communist countries, but possible all over the world—that we experience the transformation into a patrimonial capitalism where profit-seeking will be replaced by rent-seeking that is likely to damage the economic dynamism and a relatively open, socially mobile and at least to some extent merit-based society modern capitalism offered the world.

Such re-feudalization of social order has also political consequences, the spread of illiberal state. While the rise of liberal democracy in the West corresponded with the functioning of powerful checks and balances, we see increasing rejection of the liberal ideas justified with the need for strong leadership and "draining of the swamp"—as Donald Trump put it—because checks and balances make it harder to implement fast, radical decisions. We live in a world ruled increasingly by "anxiety", by fear from "others", migrants, with people whose culture is different from ours, in general from globalization (this is the topic of our last chapter). The three most powerful figures of our present world, Vladimir Putin, President Xi and Donald Trump are deeply committed to the idea of illiberalism (though Trump has to deal with a fairly powerful liberal institutions, the judiciary, the two houses of the Congress and surviving strong commitment to individual liberty even aiming some members of his own party).

References

Bourdieu, P., and J.-C. Passeron. [1970] 1977. *Reproduction in Education, Society and Culture*. London: Sage.

Conley, Dalton. 1999. *Being Black and Living in Red*. Berkeley: University of California Press.

Khan, Shamus Rahman. 2011. *Privilege: The Making of an Adolescent Elite at St. Paul's School*. Princeton: Princeton University Press.

Mitnik, Pablo, and David Grusky, et al. 2015. New Estimates on Intergenerational Mobility Using Administrative Data. IRS Working Paper, Washington, DC. www.irs.gov/pub/irs-soi/15rpintergenmobility.pdf.

Pearson, Helen. 2016. *The Life Project: The Extraordinary Story of Our Ordinary Lives*. New York: Soft Skull Press.

Piketty, Thomas. 2018. Brahmin Left vs, Merchant Right: Rising Inequality in the Changing Structure of Political Conflict. WID Working Papers Series No. 7.

Putnam, Robert D. 2015. *Our Kids: The American Dream in Crisis*. New York: Simon & Schuster.

Reeves, E.Richard. 2017. *Dream Hoarders: How the American Upper Middle Class Is Leaving Everyone Else in the Dust, Why That Is a Problem, and What to Do About It.* Washington, DC: Brookings Institution Press.

Riviera, Lauren A. 2015. *Pedigree: How Elite Students Get Elite Jobs.* Princeton: Princeton University Press.

Schwarz, Christine R., and Robert Mare. 2005. Trend in Educational Assortative Marriage from 1940 to 2003. *Demography* 42: 621–646.

Standing, Guy. 2017. *Basic Income.* New Haven: Yale University Press.

Vaughan-Whitehead, Daniel (ed.). 2016. *Europe's Disappearing Middle Class? Evidence from the World of Work.* Cheltenham, UK and Northampton, MA, USA: Edward Elgar Publishing and Geneva: International Labour Office.

CHAPTER 5

Stages of Rent-Seeking Under Post-communism

Abstract Re-feudalization or patrimonial capitalism can have a political consequence: the illiberal state, as Russia and China illustrate. Given the specific historical and geographical circumstances, as well as the variations in cultural traditions, Mihályi and Szelényi distinguish three different rent-seeking mechanisms under post-communism as times changed since 1989: market capture by political elites, state capture by oligarchs, and capture of oligarchs by autocratic rulers. The last mechanism is particularly controversial and very difficult to judge from a moral/ethical standpoint because of the widespread practice of selective criminalization of the real or potential enemies of the autocratic rulers. The Putin–Khodorkovsky war put into the limelight a particular nature of the Russian post-communist economy: its strong dependence on world market rents earned from the export of gas and oil.

Keywords Market capture · State capture · Oligarchs · Natural resource rents · Autocratic rulers · Russia · China · Poland · Hungary

The assertion that we want to prove in this chapter is that the functioning of the really powerful, but potentially dangerous post-communist countries (Russia and China) cannot be understood without a thorough inclusion of rent-seeking into their respective description model. However, when these two countries (and the East European countries)

P. Mihályi and I. Szelényi,
Rent-Seekers, Profits, Wages and Inequality,
https://doi.org/10.1007/978-3-030-03846-5_5

are paralleled to the United States, it is very imperative to see that while rent-seeking is an important feature of both systems, *the forms of rent-seeking are very different.*

Given the specific historical and geographical circumstances, as well as the variations in cultural traditions, we shall distinguish three different rent-seeking mechanisms under post-communism as times changed since 1989:

- market capture by political elites
- state capture by oligarchs and
- capture of oligarchs by autocratic rulers.

As we argued in the preceding chapters, there are some indications that Western type of capitalism may become patrimonial capitalism. In the post-communist context, we do not have the data yet to test Piketty's assertion. Nevertheless, we can accept his general hypothesis, although it is still unclear, whether the children of the highly visible present day ultra-wealthy in Russia or China will have the possibility to pass the entire set of property rights to their children—including the right to sell these assets to foreigners or move the family's financial wealth to foreign countries.[1]

Rent-seeking behavior has been historically present in all capitalist market economies, even in the most advanced ones. The early high levels of inequalities were driven by two forces (i) In European countries (especially in England), the privileged estate was able to convert its feudal privileges into privileged positions on the market; (ii) Since appropriate mechanisms of market regulations were not in place, it was possible to create monopoly situations, or to create cartel-like agreements. Good examples are the "robber barons" in the late nineteenth-century United States (Josephson 1934; Folsom 2010). Some of these robber barons came close to "state capture"[2] until state's elite fought back with anti-trust legislations.[3]

[1]We may add to the list the post-Soviet Central Asian republics, Belorussia, Ukraine, Hungary—especially, but not exclusively after 2010, Romania, Bulgaria, Serbia, Albania, Macedonia, and probably a few more countries, where the signs of patrimonial capitalism are visible.

[2]The notion of state capture was introduced by Stigler (1971).

[3]Theodore Roosevelt anti-monopoly legislation during the early 1900 is a prime example of successfully regulating and limiting rent-seeking.

Interestingly, the transition from socialism to capitalism was often driven or at least colored by similar—and often more extreme—rent-seeking behavior. Much like during the transition from feudalism to capitalism, there was an intense struggle of old elites to retain their power and convert their former privileged position into economic wealth/power. Those who were suddenly converted to the idea of free markets from central planning did not always realize that some regulation (even planning) might be needed to have genuinely free and competitive markets. Private property rights were often (and remain) ambiguous.[4] The conditions of law and order, the separation of powers, especially separation of politics from the economy was (and still is) negotiated. It could not be implemented instantly after the disintegration of socialism, and even a quarter of a century after the transition, it is still fought over intensively in many countries. Post-communist capitalism is a curious system, where in many cases (like Russia at least after 2000, in Hungary after 2010, to some extent in Poland after 2015) "*politics remains in command*", as Mao defined—quite well—the essence of socialism with this formulation.

Such institutional inertia of the transition was aggravated by a sense of urgency to convert state property into private wealth as fast as possible (not in China though). Yeltsin after 1991 committed himself to build capitalism in Russia in "500 days".[5] During the early 1990s, political elites and their economist advisors tended to believe that once identifiable owners are found for formerly state-owned firms, the free market will resolve everything else. It does not really matter who becomes the first private owner, whether the first owner buys the shares of companies from his own money or receives them in the form of a lottery or voucher-distribution. If the first owner is incompetent (or corrupt), he will be replaced through market competition by competent market actors.

[4] David Stark (1996).

[5] The so-called 500 days program was proposed in August 1990 by Grigory Yavlinsky with the support of the last Soviet leader, Mikhail Gorbachev. In essence, this was a 400-page report which called for the creation of a competitive market economy, mass privatization, prices determined by the market, integration with the world economic system, a large transfer of power from the Union government to the Republics, etc.

1 Market Capture by Political Elites

Market capture by political elites had multiple variants.

1.1 *Political Capitalism: The Use of Market Mechanisms by Communist Cadres to Turn State Property into Private Wealth*

In the early stages of privatization, it was often assumed that the former communist elite converts their political capital into economic wealth.[6] Indeed, it was seen by many commentators that post-communist capitalism was simply a "Kleptocracy" in which the political bosses stole the state assets. Undoubtedly, this occurred in large numbers in Russia,[7] Ukraine, in the Central Asian republics, and to a certain extent in Bulgaria and Romania, where the elite circulation in the first few years was minimal.

One good example is Victor Chernomyrdin. In the mid-1990s, the CIA estimated his net worth at $5 billion, but he claimed to have ownership in a few million. In 1978, he was already working at the Central Committee of the Soviet Communist Party and then back-and-forth between high government posts (deputy minister, minister of gas industry) and major managerial positions (Chairman of Gazprom). He was the Prime Minister of Russia between 1991 and 1998. He passed away in 2010 and took all his secrets into his grave.

As Hankiss (1990) and Staniszkis (1991) independently pointed out communist elites woke up early in Hungary and Poland and tried to convert state-owned enterprises (SOEs) into private firms by using the technology called "spontaneous privatization", but in 1989–1990 they lost political power.[8] As far as we can tell neither in Hungary nor in Poland succeeded the communist political leadership to accumulate substantial wealth before 1989. Nevertheless, there is a kernel of truth to the Hankiss–Staniszkis hypothesis. Some of the post-communist "new rich"

[6] This was the nomenclature bourgeoisie hypothesis of Erzsébet Szalai (1989), Elemér Hankiss (1990), and Jadwiga Staniszkis (1991).

[7] See Szelényi (2010).

[8] For an excellent comparison of Central European post-communist capitalisms, see Bohle Dorothee and Bela Greskovits (2012). However, it is important to underscore that none of the Central Europeans whose names can be found on the Forbes billionaires list are known to have been high communist party official before 1989, see Szelényi (2010).

in both countries began to accumulate capital before or just during the regime change and it turned out to be a starting point for their future wealth.[9]

1.2 Market Capture by Political Elites During Privatization of State Property for Personal Enrichment or Recruitment of Clients

When mass privatization became the official aim of governments, SOEs were passed into private hands either by vouchers[10] or they were offered for sale on competitive actions.[11] Workers, ordinary citizens, or inheritors did not know what to do with vouchers, so they sold them to risk-tolerant young investors under daily changing market conditions. But markets do not come from a thin air, as we know from Polanyi (1944). Also in these cases, markets were created by states and/or by political elites. Such a "management" or even "creation" of markets was inevitable for domestic, and even for foreign investors.

Let us begin with domestic investors. During communist times private ownership was outlawed, hence accumulation of private capital was very limited. To enable at least some domestic investors to purchase state property, it had to be underpriced. Domestic investors—who did not have any reliable track record or credit rating—needed government supported bank loans. This required a preselection to be allowed to make bids on auctions. Preselection, that is inevitable, relied on possession of personal or political capital. In countries, where communist elites survived (like in China) or where the new elites monopolized political

[9] In Poland, for instance, Jan Weichert and Mariusz Walter—major owners of post-communist media—were suspected to have started their business while working for the Polish security services, though they vehemently denied this accusation. In Hungary, Sándor Demján, one of the wealthiest Hungarian during post-communist times (who passed away in 2018 as a very wealthy man), started his career as a manager of successful cooperative (i.e. semi-private) ventures in the 1980s. László Kapolyi was a high official during communist times and was listed among the wealthiest Hungarians after 2000 (see Kolosi and Szelényi 2010). By the time of his death in 2014, however, he lost virtually everything.

[10] Vouchers were handed out either for compensation of property lost under communism—like in Hungary, the Baltic states, etc.—or as a share of workers, or citizens in public wealth a method used in Czechoslovakia, Russia, and many other countries.

[11] Until 1995, Hungary pursued privatization through open tenders and IPOs, in which foreign investors competed with each other. See Edal et al. (1998), Mihályi (2001), and King and Szelényi (2005).

positions (like in Russia, Bulgaria, or Romania), the former (or in China still active) communist cadres had advantages.

China is a special case since market transition in China has been taking place all along until the present day, under the rule of the Communist Party. According to the evidence we could find[12] during the first two decades of the reform, wealth accumulation was mainly or exclusively driven "from below". By the year 2000, virtually all Chinese billionaires came from a humble background, started as rice farmers or bricklayers. Privatization of large SOEs started around 1997 and there is some evidence that during the past decade or so some high communist party cadres and their family did become ultra-wealthy.[13] The manipulation of markets served either the personal economic interest of the new (or old, surviving) political elites, or the elite may use it as a mechanism to recruit and retain clients. All political elites need clients, but this is especially important if a regime—like most post-communist ones, even the Russian—wants to retain at least the semblance of democracy and faces at least apparently competitive elections.

The recent Russian history had partly similar examples, when the wealthiest businessmen started from relatively unimportant (though not humble) positions.[14] These figures were "initiated" into the new grand bourgeoisie since they were expected to be talented and loyal in exchange for "managed auctions" as described above. Valery Streletsky told in an interview to Klebnikov (2001): "The key factor in the privatization process was the attitude of Tatyana Dyachenko [Yeltsin's beloved daughter] to this or that banker/oligarch. (…) She would go to the President and say: this man is good man and that man is bad man. This should be supported and that should not be supported. (…)

[12]See *The Forbes* list and *Hurun* list of Chinese billionaires, see Szelényi (2010).

[13]There are contradictory assessments of the personal wealth of former Prime Minister Wen Jiabao and current President Xi Jinping. The New York Times reported on both of them that their family wealth may be in the range of $1–2 billion dollars. If there is wealth in the Xi family, most of it was made by the President's daughter, Qi Qiaoqiao and her husband Deng Jiagui. It is also rumored that many large nominally state-owned firms, whose CEO's are "princelings", hence children of former "revolutionary heroes" (President Xi is one of them) are, in reality, entirely privately owned. (Personal communication by Lu Peng.)

[14]Vladimir Potanin—who invented the debt-swap scheme—was among the few high government officials who were not hiding. He was listed among the dollar billionaires after 1991.

Tatyana Dyachenko is the only person the President listens".[15] Boris Berezovsky[16] and Roman Abramovich[17] are prime examples of people who acquired substantial wealth mainly due to their contemporary personal rather than previous political connections.

But these "grants" given to the new grand bourgeoisie which was "appointed" by the political boss, anticipated some return to the boss. Indeed, in exchange of Yeltsin's contribution to his growth as a businessmen in 1996, when a Communist Party candidate represented a real threat to Yeltsin's reelection, Berezovsky not only supported the Yeltsin campaign, but managed to persuade six other "oligarchs", the wealthiest of the wealthy at that time, the so-called Big Seven to push for the President's reelection. Next to Berezovsky other members of

[15] Ibid., pp. 202–203.

[16] Boris Berezovsky (1946–2013) was one of the first and the most prominent founding member of the club of newly emergent oligarchs. He earned, in 1983, a Ph.D. in mathematics and at the Soviet Academy of Sciences, he became director of one of the laboratories of the Institute of Management. As far as we can tell, there is no indication that Berezovsky was close to high-ranking Soviet party officials. He had good relationship with the young reformers, Yegor Gaidar, Anatoly Chubais, and Valentin Yumashev. Yumashev was a journalist—eventually became Yeltsin's chief of staff and the second husband of Tanya (or Tatyana) Yeltsin—but during the early 1990s, he was just a ghostwriter for the President. He helped Yeltsin to write his 1989 book and was helping him with the "*Notes of a President*"—eventually published in 1994. It was Yumashev who introduced Berezovsky to Tatyana, who at that time was the wife of Dyachenko (a commodity trader, who became at one point Berezovsky's business partner in Sibneft), but already a good friend of Yumashev. With his newly acquired contacts, Berezovsky managed to take major managerial positions and eventually ownership in the car manufacturing firm Avtovaz, in the Russian national airline, Aeroflot, the major oil company Sibneft. His economic empire also included the aluminum industry and some important media outlets. In 1995, he also acquired TV Channel 1, the most commonly watched TV station which had a tremendous impact on public opinion in the country.

[17] Another of these young "talents" discovered by Tatyana was Roman Abramovich. He started out in the shadow economy. It is rumored that he started out his business activities during the late 1980s by selling plastic ducks out of his Moscow apartment and working as a street trader. In 1993, he met Berezovsky, who liked him and introduced him to the "family". In 1995, in the loans-for-shares program the two men acquired Sibneft. Abramovich paid something like $80 million for the whole company, which must have been worth several billion already at that time. Eventually, he even moved to live inside the Kremlin and became a close friend of Yeltsin's daughter Tatyana Yeltsin, who often spent time at Abramovich's dacha. So this is indeed something like the "adopted family", a term coined by Magyar (2016) explaining his theory of the "mafia state". It is noteworthy that Klebnikov used this term already for Yeltsin, in the year 2000.

the Big Seven were: Mikhail Fridman, Vladimir Vinogradov, Mikhail Khodorkovsky,[18] Vladimir Gusinsky, Vladimir Potanin, and Aleksander Smolinsky. The Big Seven claimed already in 1996, just five years after the collapse of the USSR, that they owned half of Russia.[19]

1.3 Manipulating Markets After Privatization Either to Serve the Enrichment of New Political Elites or to Recruit New Loyal Propertied Bourgeoisie

The suspicion that political office holders use their office for personal enrichment is still seriously considered as the main feature of the new system. We have already mentioned the name of Bálint Magyar (2016), a trained sociologist and former Hungarian minister in two Socialist-Liberal coalition governments during the 1990s and early 2000s, who characterized the right-wing FIDESZ government after 2010 as "*Mafia state*". In his model, Mr. Orbán, the Hungarian Prime Minister acts as "god-father". It is claimed that government contracts and EU subsidized programs are allocated to family members or members of Orbán's "adopted family", hence to loyal clients. Magyar didn't hesitate for a moment to claim that his model applies to Yeltsin's and Putin's Russia as well.[20]

There are many ways markets can be influenced after privatization was completed. Arguably, the most important or one of the most important mechanisms is the manipulation of public procurements which by law require competition open to all. Some sectors are particularly suitable for such manipulations (e.g. road constructions, IT services, commercial advertisements of SOEs). By governmental decree such purchases can be declared to be "emergent", hence they shortcut complicated

[18] Klebnikov (2001) offers a crisp description of his trajectory: Khodorkovsky had a classic career path of a Yeltsin–era business magnate. In 1987, as a top leader of Moscow's Communist Youth League, he established a trading cooperative financed with communist Party money; the next year he established a bank. In 1990–1993, Khodorkovsky entered the Russian government, serving first as economic advisor to the Russian Prime Minister and then as deputy minister of fuel and energy. In 1999 Khodorkovsky was listed as the 5th wealthiest person in Russia, with an estimated wealth of $500 million.

[19] The Big Seven—Russia's Financial Empires, www.worldbank.org/html/prddr/trans/feb98/bigseven.htm.

[20] In 2016, Magyar's book was published in Russia, too. The English-language edition came out in the same year.

competition and give contracts to clients (occasionally they may be even proxies to government officials). Without competitive bidders, or with reduced number of bidders the price for the services the government contracts can be way above what would have been in free competition, therefore who wins such bids collect substantial rent over the profit they would have made on real markets.[21] The government can also limit rewarding licenses, for instance which radio station or TV channel can use frequencies most often listened to or watched.

As the Yeltsin example illustrated, the funding of electoral campaigns needs wealthy supporters who finance the campaign directly and indirectly through the media. Such deals could have been the source of personal income for political bosses like President Putin or Prime Minister Orbán in Hungary.[22] A rather trivial case to collect a large number of supporters was the allocation of tobacco shop licenses in Hungary. Prior to that, virtually all stores (including food stores and gas stations) could sell tobacco and a substantial part of their revenue comes from this trade. In 2013, the government created special tobacco stores, which acquired the exclusive right to sell tobacco, transferring "rent" from all other sales points to the newly licensed tobacco stores. This was not a major source of income. Nevertheless, it created a 20-year monopoly for some small, medium size businessmen, who according to at least to opposition politicians were loyal supporters of the government.

Of course, such manipulation of markets is well-known in all countries (a famous example is public purchases of military equipment in the United States), but as we showed above, these practices are especially widespread in the post-communist economies. This is not only our

[21] For an empirical study of the situation in Romania, see Pirvu (2015).

[22] Vladimir Putin's personal wealth is subject of wild speculations. Some commentators claim he is the wealthiest man in the world with a personal property $40–70 billion. Putin's official disclosure acknowledges his property to be worth of $119,000 (he owns two apartments and one garage place). There are also similarly wild—and unconfirmed—speculations about private wealth of Hungarian Prime Minister, Viktor Orbán. The personal wealth of current political office holders may be overestimated by political opponents. In any case, smart political bosses do not accumulate wealth in their own name, but pass it on to their extended family of friends. Hence if Putin indeed managed to accumulate some wealth of his own, it may be under the name of her daughter Yekaterina and her husband (it is reported the couple owns $2.83 billion just in Silberg Company). Putin's friend, the cellist Sergei Roldugin is also believed to act as his surrogate when he was reported to move billions of dollars in Panama.

opinion; this is one of the reasons why these countries are labeled "corrupt" by Transparency International. Ironically, EU money to help the new (post-communist) member states did more harm in this respect than the progress emanating from newly built transparency mechanism arising from EU membership.

2 State Capture by Oligarchs

State capture by business elites is most often seen as cases of rent-seeking (and corruption) in non/post/communist emergent markets, for instance in the late nineteenth-century United States or the twentieth- and twenty-first- century Africa. Such rent-seeking behavior exists under post-communism, but it is relatively rare, given the weakness of propertied bourgeoisie and its dependence on the political elite. Those who managed to capture the state in the late nineteenth century United States were called "robber barons", their prime example being Rockefeller, Vanderbilt, or Jay Gould. In the post-communist world, they are called oligarchs.

The notion of oligarch is disputed. In this book we call oligarchs those super wealthy individuals who managed to "privatize the state" itself (to use again Klebnikov's term). Hence, these are individuals who did not become wealthy because they occupied political positions or were believed to be loyal followers of political bosses, but who managed to use their wealth to capture the state itself. They were not unlike the "boyars" of early tsarist Russia, a class of wealthy individuals who used politics and the state to gain wealth rather than the other way around. It is only Russia by the end of the Yeltsin years, when we can see cases of such state capture by the new wealthy.

As the Russian state began to collapse, the largest business conglomerates began to buildup their own armed security force occasionally with as many as 1000 mercenaries.[23] Indeed, large businessmen needed security forces, since the city of Moscow was ruled by mafia, usually run either by Russians or Chechens, and without getting protection from one or the other life was virtually impossible for such business figures. Unsurprisingly, two such figures Gusinsky, protected by Russians and Berezovsky, protected by Chechens suspected each other to be behind

[23] Klebnikov, p. 151, also *Washington Post*, April 7, 1995.

assassination attempt against them and plot to get them arrest by law enforcement agencies until the two giant oligarchs around 1996 sat down and agreed to cooperate with each other rather than try to destroy one another.

Berezovsky comes the closest to be called an "oligarch". After the 1996 reelection of Yeltsin as President, he became involved in state affairs, for a while he served as Deputy Secretary of the National Security Council in charge of Chechnya. Since some of his bodyguards were Chechens he had working relations with the Islamist leaders of Chechen uprising. Even after he left this position, he continued negotiations to free hostages taken by Chechen rebels. So he used his business success to gain substantial political power, even political office and many commentators—like Klebnikov—assumed he might have used this office to further his personal enrichment.

3 Capture of Oligarchs by Autocratic Rulers

In 2000, Berezovsky and some other (still surviving members) of the Big Seven (namely Khodorkovsky and Fridman) supported Putin's election, sort of were bringing Putin "into the family"—to use the Mafia language. But Putin was no Yeltsin. He wanted to be Peter, the Great and did not want to be bossed around by the "boyars"—i.e. the oligarchs. Though Berezovsky was elected to Duma (the Russian legislature) in 1999, he soon clashed with Putin and fled to England. Later he was sentenced to prison *in absentia* and was accused of various murders.[24] Berezovsky became Public Enemy Number One for Putin's Russia—it is rumored that there were several attempts by Russian agents to murder him in London.[25] He passed away in 2013 under unclear circumstances. He might have been killed by Russian intelligence services, or he might have lost so much his previous wealth (most to Abramovich) that he did not want to readjust his life to be "poor", so he rather committed suicide. Much like Berezovsky, Mikhail Khodorkovsky was also far too ambitious politically for Putin. Probably he sensed trouble with the new

[24]While no murder charges were proven against him in any fair court of justice, he was suspected to be involved in the murder of Vlad Listyev, Russia's most successful TV producer four years earlier. Listyev supported the privatization of TV 1 to Berezovsky, but he advocated a fair competition for advertising time, that clashed with Berezovsky's interest.

[25]*The Times*, July 18, 2007.

political boss, so in early 2003 he proposed to merge his own oil company, Yukos with another major Russian firm, Sibneft. As Berezovsky had to escape Russia, he passed ownership of Sibneft to Roman Abramovich (a solid #2 on the list of wealthiest Russian even in 2009), who regarded Berezovsky as his mentor. In 2003, Khodorkovsky was put on trial for corruption and sent behind bars. He was only released in 2013 when he moved to Switzerland with a small part of his former wealth (in 1999 he was believed to own $500 million, today, his assets are estimated to be around $100 million). While Khodorkovsky was "eliminated" by Putin, Abramovich is a survivor. This may be due to the fact that unlike Berezovsky or Khodorkovsky, he kept a low profile and assured Putin of his unconditional loyalty. As a "reward", he sort of "inherited" a great deal of property from his former mentor/friend turned into a bitter enemy of Berezovsky.

Excessive rent-seeking threatens the legitimacy of the regimes and even private ownership. In response, political elites launch anti-corruption campaigns. But it remains to be seen whether the anti-corruption drive is indeed aiming at reducing rent-seeking or it is merely an instrument to remove political enemies and to reallocate the wealth of oligarchs whose loyalty cannot be trusted. Khodorkovsky was jailed for charges in corruption, but it is hard not to see political motives behind the Putin–Khodorkovsky war. So it is possible that these corruption charges are instruments in a **selective criminalization** of enemies. The line between fighting graft and purging political opponents is blurred. Many members of the economic and political post-communist elites are likely to have "skeletons" in their closets. Businessmen under post-communist conditions—given the ambiguities of legal regulations and private ownership—may be even more likely to offer their gratitude (bribes?) to political office-holders than in more established liberal democracies and the political elite may be more inclined to accept appreciations of their services (take bribes?). There are many candidates to be chosen as "corrupt", the question is who will at the end be selected.

The Putin–Khodorkovsky war put into the limelight a particular nature of the Russian post-communist economy: it's strong dependence on world market rents earned from the export of gas and oil (and other minerals) (Fig. 1).

In fact, as Table 1 in the next chapter, Russia is the only world power the fate of which is significantly influenced by natural resource rents. When international energy prices are high and rising, there is a strong temptation on *any* Russian leader to halt or slow down the enrichment

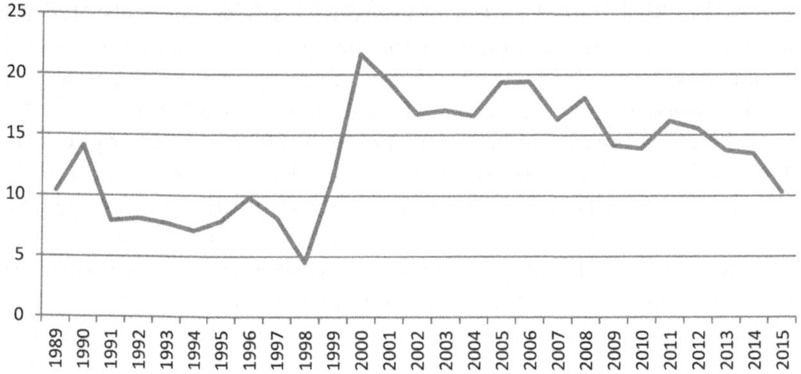

Fig. 1 The relative size of natural resource rent in the Russian economy, as a percentage of its GDP (*Note and source* See Table 1 in Chapter 6)

of the energy barons. When prices go down and the rent component of the export prices is shrinking, the shortfalls of the state budget "force" the leader to renationalize the firms controlling energy production. From the perspective of the state, this is the cynical message to the oil and gas barons: *Heads I Win, Tails You Lose.*

In 2012, when the Communist Party of China transferred the power from President Hu to President Xi, the authorities promised to catch "tigers and flies" in a newly launched anticorruption campaign. So far they did catch quite a few flies and some tigers, but those tigers look too much as political enemies to those in the highest position of political power. The first tiger to fall victim to the anticorruption campaign was Bo Xilai. Bo was the first Secretary of the Communist Party of Chongqing, the largest city in the world and an aspirant for a position in the Standing Committee of the Politbureau. He was a Maoism inspired left populist politician. He kept speculators out of the urban land market and used the profit gained this way to build public housing schools and improve medical facilities.[26] People had to sing songs from the times of the Cultural Revolution, but they received better services. So, he looked far too popular and dangerous for the Beijing establishment. He was certainly no saint, but his selection as the first "tiger" may have more to do with his candidacy for the Standing Committee of the Politbureau rather than his deep involvement in corruption. The case

[26] See Huang (2011) on the Chongqing model.

against Bo Xilai started with a trial against his wife, Gu Kailai. Gu was accused and eventually sentenced for life for the murder of an English business associate, Neil Heywood. She might have been the murderer, but Heywood's body was cremated right after his death. Nevertheless, it took the court only seven hours on August 9, 2012 to find her guilty and sentenced her to life imprisonment.[27] Just 11 months after her trial, Bo was also put on trial for corruption and abuse of office powers. He was accused and found guilty to have received $3.6 million bribes from two local businessmen. He might very well have taken those bribes, but what is curious why top party leaders, whose families' fortune is in the billions of dollars, are *not* being investigated. Ironically, the successor of Bo in the regional party leadership and a member of the Politbureau, Sun Zhengcai had exactly the same fate in 2017. He was first removed from his elected party position for "grave violation of discipline", and then he was accused of plotting against the communist party and expelled from it. In early 2018, he was charged with bribery by the People's Procuratorate.

Selective criminalization and "capturing" the *nouveau riche* is not an exclusively Russian or Chinese phenomenon. Some commentators suspect the anti-corruption drive under President Johannis in Romania may be also politically motivated and there is little doubt that witch-hunting was also used widely in Hungary, especially after 2010. The new center-right government accused many former socialist and liberal politicians of corruption and quite a few after spending a long time in "pre-trial detention" were found not guilty by the relatively still independent courts. There is at least one very interesting case to move against a "new rich"—which was perceived and was probably indeed disloyal—by the Hungarian government. Mr. Lajos Simicska, the former treasurer of the post-2010 Hungarian ruling party, a previous winner of many "restricted" competition for government contracts, hence a great rent collector, suddenly lost the personal trust of the Prime Minister at the end of 2014. In few weeks he was excluded from public procurement tenders, his media firms lost government advertisements. Most recently even his hunting plot, which he rented from a state-owned forest farm, was taken away from him. As the Prime minister put it astutely: "The trees cannot grow into the skies". Unlike Khodorkovsky, Simicska didn't

[27]Without a body and murder weapon one would have expected a somewhat longer trial. She confessed, but for murder the usual sentence in China is capital punishment and she got away with a life sentence.

get into jail, but his business empire got into serious troubles, he never won a large public procurement tender anymore. At the very end, in the Summer of 2018, he was forced to sell all his business assets to a politically less committed right-wing fellow businessman.

References

Bohle, Dorothee, and Béla Greskovits. 2012. *Capitalist Diversity on Europe's Periphery*. Ithaca and London: Cornell University Press.

Erzsébet, Szalai. 1989. The New Elite. *Across Frontiers* 5: 25–31.

Eyal, Gil, Iván Szelényi, and E. Townsley. 1998. *Making Capitalism Without Capitalists*. London: Verso.

Folsom, Burton W. [1987] 2010. *The Myth of the Robber Barons*. Herndon, VA: Young America's Foundation.

Hankiss, Elemér. 1990. *East European Alternatives*. Oxford: Clarendon Press.

Huang, P. 2011. Chongqing: Equitable Development Driven by a 'Third Hand'? *Modern China* 6: 559–622.

Josephson, M. 1934. *The Robber Barons*. New York: Harcourt.

King, L., and Iván Szelényi. 2005. Post-communist Economic Systems. In *The Handbook of Economic Sociology*, ed. S. Neil and R. Swedberg, 206–232. Princeton: Princeton University Press.

Klebnikov, P. 2001. *Godfather of the Kremlin*. New York: Houghton Mifflin Harcourt.

Kolosi, Tamás, and Iván Szelényi. 2010. *Hogyan legyünk milliárdosok?* Budapest: Corvina (In Hungarian).

Magyar, Bálint. 2016. *Post-communist Mafia State*. Budapest: Central European University Press.

Mihályi, Péter. 2001. The Evolution of Hungary's Approach to FDI in Post-communist Privatization. *Transnational Corporations* 3: 61–74.

Pirvu, D. 2015. Corruption: Profile of Political Companies in Romania. *Acta Oeconomica* 65 (Special Issue) (1): 65–82.

Polanyi, Karl. 1944. *The Great Transformation*. New York: Farrar and Rinehart.

Staniszkis, J. 1991. Political Capitalism in Poland. *East European Politics and Societies* 1: 127–141.

Stark, David. 1996. Recombinant Property in East European Capitalism. *American Journal of Sociology* 101 (4): 492–504.

Stigler, George. 1971. The Theory of Economic Regulation. *The Bell Journal of Economics and Management Science* 2 (Spring) (1): 3–21.

Szelényi, Iván. 2010. The New Grand Bourgeoisie Under Post-communism. Central Europe, Russia and China Compared. Working Paper No. 2010/63. United Nations University, Helsinki, World Institute for Development Economic Research.

CHAPTER 6

Rent-Securing by the Nation-States and Rent Destruction by Globalization

Abstract We live in an epoch when forces of globalization, free cross-national movement of capital, goods and labor have been gaining ground, but at the same time, they are being met with increasing resistance by nation-states. Rents became suddenly visible and thus undeniable, as third parties like the Chinese or Indian workers claimed them at the expense of shareholders and workers in the core countries. This chapter is focusing on this rent-destructing impact of globalization. In 2016, Donald Trump won the elections to a large extent by votes from white workers who lost jobs or had to accept lower incomes due to globalization and immigration, which in turn led to the fast improvement of living standards in many other parts of the world (including Eastern Europe and Russia).

Keywords Global inequalities · Anti-globalization movements · Protectionism · Anti-migration ideologies · Multi-culturalism · Rent-destruction

In the last decades of the twentieth and first decades of the early twenty-first century we live in an epoch when forces of globalization, free cross-national, nearly global movement of capital, goods and labor have been gaining ground, but at the same time, they are being met with increasing resistance by nation-states. For a while, it appeared that the march of the European Union towards a federal European United

P. Mihályi and I. Szelényi,
Rent-Seekers, Profits, Wages and Inequality,
https://doi.org/10.1007/978-3-030-03846-5_6

States (and expansion further in Eastern and Southern Europe) is not only unstoppable, but is being complemented with a trans-Atlantic free trade treaty, and an American-Pacific free trade zone. Even Russia tried to implement a Euro-Asian equivalent of the EU. Capital was flowing around the world with little constraints; tariffs on export/import on goods were shrinking if not disappearing. The migration of people driven both by political/military conflicts and the desire to find a country, which may offer them more freedom and a better life, began to match the peaks of earlier migration waves in history. Though the freedom of labor to move never matched, or never came close to the freedom of capital to move around the world.

The struggle between globalism and anti-globalism cannot merely be cast as a conflict between left and right, between liberals and conservatives. Jeremy Corbyn—with spotless left-wing and liberal credentials—in the UK was accused by mainstream Labor Party members not having campaigned forcefully against Brexit and hence helped right-wing conservatives to gain the anti-EU vote. In the United States, Bernie Sanders on the question of anti-globalism, even on defending some US industries with a tariff, was on identical wavelengths with Donald Trump and most Republican members of both houses of the Congress.

Essentially the **anti-globalization movement** is driven by the argument/belief that national sovereignty has to be defended against the destructive forces of globalization. Representatives on the right-wing conservative (and occasionally liberal) side attack the global order for being led by self-serving international super-state bureaucracy. For some left-leaning liberals, globalization serves the interest of multi-national companies. These criticisms of globalization are not without substance. The attack on "Brussel's bureaucrats" with little political legitimacy is not without foundations. Multinationals and the free flow of capital often destroy high quality small domestic businesses; flood countries with low quality, mass-produced goods and destroy formerly well-paid jobs.[1] These blames have to be articulated, but we leave this task to others. In this book, which is focusing on the often unintended and undesired consequences of rent-seeking behavior, we emphasize the **rent-destructing impact of globalization**, as a result of the free flow of capital, goods and labor.

[1] Stiglitz (2002, pp. 5–9).

Our point of departure is the analysis of the role of the nation-state. Nation-states, based on the belief of common ancestry, culture and language—which were largely absent in pre-capitalist empires—emerged at the relatively early stages of capitalist development, the prime example being the French revolution. One of the critical functions of the nation-states was to promote national development. Protectionism was one of the tools to achieve this. An early critic of such economic policy was Adam Smith who saw the advantages of the British world empire for capitalist development. The only time when he uses the term "invisible hand"[2]—which refers to the unrestricted role of free markets—in *The Wealth of Nations* occurs in the discussion of international trade. He was a firm believer that greatest efficiency can be achieved in international trade where capital flows to countries, where it can be the most efficiently employed and tariff imposed on the movement of goods only support inefficient domestic industries. Smith is also clear in stating labor also should be moving freely. People should move freely around the world—much like capital or goods—and make a living wherever they can use their labor more effectively.

We follow Smith in this respect; we only emphasize more than most of his interpreters the value of free flow of labor. Nevertheless, in Adam Smith time, when labor was abundant in Britain (the enclosure movement was still underway, agrarian labor was still transferred to urban industry), the movement of labor was not an issue as important as it is today. We suggest in this chapter that today free (which does not mean uncontrolled) migration is a major component of free (and social) market economies. As of the second decade of the twenty-first century, the protection of the "nation" against migration, especially by culturally and/or ethnically different migrants is becoming #1 issue of social policy by nationalist be they be from the political right or left, be they be

[2] Interestingly in the works of Smith, the word "invisible hand" appears only three times. Once in *The Wealth of Nations*, so often cited by neo-classical economists where it indeed means unregulated markets. But he already used this term in his first book *The Theory of Moral Sentiments*. There it was the "Hand of God" and referred to the importance of compassion. People seek sympathy in interacting with others, hence "self-interest" is in no contradiction with the interest of others. Whether Smith changed his mind while writing *The Wealth of Nations* and narrowed interest to "economic self-interest" is hotly debated in the Smith literature. It is, however, clear while Smith vehemently opposed to tariffs but he might not have shared the verdict of neo-liberals, namely that "the state is the problem, not the solution"—to cite Ronald Reagan.

liberals or conservatives. While inequality used to be the hottest topic some years ago, now it seems to be replaced by migration, a win-win topic at democratic elections.

Protectionism both by keeping domestic capital at home and keeping foreign produced goods abroad by tariffs is complemented by keeping "migrants" out. All of these policies, we will argue in this last substantive chapter, is a mechanism to secure rent and the income of rent-seekers at "home", in the nation-state. This mechanism reduces the efficiency of the global economy and potentially undermines political and social security from a direction few people could have imagined say 10 years ago.

Globalization tends to have different consequences on social inequality within countries and across countries. During the past few decades, we can observe significant increase of inequalities within countries (and that can be attributed to the rent-destructing impact of globalization), but the story is more complicated in a cross-country comparison. If we do not weight by the number of inhabitants there is a trend for increased inequality in cross-national comparison (mainly attributable to the high level of poverty in small states, especially in Africa). But if we weight the size of population we have seen over the past few decades a substantial decline of inequality (mainly attributable to the drastic reduction of poverty in China and massive growth of the middle class in India).

1 Within-Country and Cross-Country Inequalities—The Links to Growth

There is one more dimension of the interpretation of within-country inequalities—the one, which preoccupied a significant weight in Piketty's two-class model, namely the *falling share of wages* within total output since the 1970s. More precisely, according to his calculations, in 1975 the share of profits in the national income was between 15 and 25% in the large, advanced OECD economies, then this share rose to 25–35% between 2000 and 2010.[3] Without questioning the validity of these estimates, it is important to underscore that a 10 percentage point decline in the share of wages is not insignificant, but its long-term consequences on workers' real wages dwarf to that of a sustained *innovation-based*

[3] See Piketty (2014), op. cit., Figure 6.5. The countries listed here are as follows: US, Japan, Germany, France, UK, Italy, Canada and Australia.

productivity increase, if this is (at least partly) reflected in the long-run growth of real wages.

Consider the following three arithmetic examples—one for the developed economies, one for developing ones and a third one in which a developed and an underdeveloped economy are contrasted.[4] Let us start with the developed economy example, with an 80:20 divide of output (GDP or Y), between real wages (W) and profits (Π) in t_0. Whether profits include some rents or not we leave aside for the moment. Assume that wages are now rising for 30 years with an annual rate of 2.0% due to the increase in labor productivity. Profits will grow at a similar rate, thus the division of output remains unchanged. In t_{30}, the level of real wages will stand at 145, a *less* than 2 times increase relative to the starting point.[5] If, by contrast, wages rise faster (say 2.7% in every year), while productivity of labor and profits grow even faster (say 4.6%) after 30 years, the share of W is bound to decrease within GDP. With these parameters, by t_{30} we shall arrive at a division of 70:30%—i.e. the share of wages will fall by 10 percentage points, as in the historical data calculated by Piketty.[6] In this second case, however, the W level will stand at 178, rather than 145—a more than ***doubled*** level as compared to t_0. Thus, workers are better off in the second case.

Now let us see the example illustrating the case of a developing economy, where it is reasonable to assume higher labor productivity growth and bigger initial inequality. We start with a 60:40 divide and forecast the W level after 30 years. If wages and profits rise in line with labor productivity of 3.0%, in t_{30} the real wages will stand at 146—i.e. 2.4 times higher than at t_0.[7] If, however, wages are rising by 4.6% per annum, but workers get less than they "deserve", because labor productivity and profits rise by 6.0% by t_{30}, the divide of output will be 50:50—i.e. once again 10 percentage point worse from the workers' perspective.

[4]We are grateful to our Hungarian colleague, Prof. István Dedák for suggesting this type of illustration.

[5]$80 \times (1 + 0.02)^{30} \approx 144.9 \quad 144.9/80 = 1.8.$

[6]$80 \times (1 + 0.04565)^{30} \approx 178.4 \quad 20 \times (1 + 0.0271)^{30} \approx 76.3$

$Y = 178.4 + 76.3 = 254.7 \quad W/Y = 30\% \ \Pi/Y = 70\%.$

[7]$60 \times (1 + 0.03)^{30} \approx 145.6 \quad 145.66/60 = 2.4.$

Nevertheless, given these parameters, in t_{30} the level of real wages will be at 233, an almost 4 times increase (!) relative to the starting point.[8]

178 vs. 145 or 233 vs. 146 represent big differences of income for workers living in both developed and developing economies, respectively. And this is what really matters for most workers: persistently and speedily rising productivity means the ability to consume more and through that, it leads to more meaningful lives.[9] This depends entirely on incomes, or on real wages as in our numeric examples. Of course, what we see here in this simple numerical exercises is nothing else, but an illustration of the infamous slogan "*Rising tide lifts all boats*". The bigger the tide, the better is for the wage earners' "boat". Why should they care much about other peoples' "boats"?

In the third example, a developed and an underdeveloped country are compared with a division of per capita output of 8000:2000 and 800:200, respectively. Thus, the developed country is 10 times more developed in terms of per capita GDP (10,000 USD/head vs. 1000 USD/head). In the richer country, wages, profits and GDP grow by 2% annually for 30 years, as in the previous cases. In the poor country, wage growth is 5%, while labor productivity rises by 8% per annum. Given the difference in growth rates of the two components of GDP, in t_{30} the new split of the national income will be less favorable to wage earners, 63:37 instead of 80:20 at t_0. However, given the higher growth rates, the poorer country will catch-up significantly in relative per capita GDP—from 10 to 30%, and in terms of wage levels from 10 to 24%.

As these unpretentious numerical exercises show, there are intrinsic links among the three most important features of capitalist market economies. Challenging Piketty's main political message János Kornai (2016) explained very convincingly what these three features are. Trivially, the first basic characteristics of capitalism is *private ownership*, which gives rise to strong incentive mechanisms that encourage both owners and managers to innovate and to accumulate, rather than using profits for luxurious consumption. The second feature, a consequence of the first

[8] $60 \times (1 + 0.0463)^{30} \approx 233.3 \quad 40 \times (1 + 0.0605)^{30} \approx 233.0$

$$W/Y = 50\% \quad \Pi/Y = 50\% \quad 233/60 = 3.9.$$

[9] For a general overview of the relevance of productivity differences among countries, see Lewis (2004) splendid book. William Lewis, director emeritus of the McKinsey Global Institute, drew on extensive microeconomic studies of 13 nations, conducted over 12 years by the Institute itself.

one, is *innovation*, and creative destruction leading to the unstoppable rise of productivity. *Inequality* is the third feature, of course, which may or may not change spectacularly in time, as illustrated in the numerical examples above through the division of national income. We are deeply convinced that in the political economy discourse it is impossible to understand the inequalities in income (and wealth) properly, if the three above-mentioned features of modern capitalism are divorced from each other and thus the specificities of distribution are considered more important than the specifics of production.

Nevertheless, while it is clear that under simplified textbook conditions economic growth and increased productivity should reduce inequality both within countries and cross-nationally, neither of that happened. We observe increased inequality within countries (there are some losers of economic growth) and cross-nationally (there are also country losers) and this is intimately linked to the complex effects of globalization. The explanation is that globalization tends to create rents for multinational companies, core countries benefit, peripheral countries lose out because of this. But globalization also destroys rents both within the core countries and given the large rise of some previously peripheral countries towards the core it also reduces the rents core countries collected before from the periphery. When we look at the complex picture, we see as a result, that globalization increases inequality in core countries, but it reduces global inequalities.

2 Global Inequalities—The Links to Globalization

Until the dawn of globalization in the mid-twentieth century, inequalities were usually seen as being local, within-country phenomenon. Ordinary people didn't know much about other countries. The within-country inequalities as we asserted at the beginning of our book, were based chiefly on ethnic, religious, racial, and gender criteria (inborn, visibly discriminative, but objective). Inequalities by class are also real and important today, but to the extent, they occur at competitive markets and are not the result of market-failures (monopolies or cartels), there is not much problem with them. In fact, some of the consequences of such inequalities are largely corrected in liberal democracies according to proper procedures: collective bargaining and free elections among parties expressing various class interests.

Marx himself was "internationalist". For him—who had limited information about the countries on the periphery—the solution to the problem of within-country inequalities was the world revolution with its center in the most developed countries. Later Marxists tended to emphasize that the solution to the worldwide nature of inequality should come from the periphery. An early example was Lenin's theory of imperialism (1916). This line of argument gained new strength with André Gunder Frank's (1966) dependency theory and Immanuel Wallerstein's (1974) world system theory. Both Frank and the early Wallerstein saw the solution in anti-systemic forces, isolation from the world system and world markets. Wallerstein (1974) identified even North Korea once as a positive model. What they did not see, that globalization can become the engine of decreasing inequality—the major, though a somewhat qualified claim of this chapter and of the whole of our book.

In the present day context, globalization also means that the share of cross-border transactions (both in goods and capital) is substantial and growing, and therefore exports and imports have a significant influence on worldwide wage levels. Wages go up in China, although they are still low in relative terms. But low wages in China, in turn, exert pressure on wages in the wealthier countries. Theoretically, this had been already taken into consideration 250 years ago. In a private correspondence with a friend and business partner David Hume (1711–1776), a Scottish philosopher, historian, and economist formulated the main line of causation like this: "The distance of China is a physical impediment to the communication, by reducing our commerce to a few commodities; and by heightening the price of these commodities, on account of the long voyage, the monopolies and the taxes. A Chinese works for three-halfpence a day, and is very industrious. Were he as near us as France or Spain, everything we use would be Chinese, till money and prices came to a level; that is, to such a level as is proportioned to the numbers of people, industry, and commodities of both countries".[10]

It should be noted that while cross-country differences are still gigantic today—and some authors claim that even growing—inequality among individuals on the global scene has declined due to the rapid economic growth in the most populous countries, such as China and India. So if we weight countries by their population globalization, in fact, led to

[10]We are grateful to our Hungarian colleague, Prof. Aladár Madarász for drawing our attention to this quote.

Table 1 The relative Size of natural resource rents in GDP: the most affected countries in 2015

In percentage			
Liberia	46.4	Central African Republic	15.4
Kuwait	39.1	Niger	14.8
Congo, Dem. Rep.	34.0	Zambia	14.4
Iraq	28.6	Ethiopia	14.3
Togo	24.7	Uganda	13.5
Guinea	24.5	Azerbaijan	13.4
Sierra Leone	23.5	Gabon	13.1
Saudi Arabia	23.4	Chad	13.1
Congo, Rep.	23.3	Mozambique	13.1
Solomon Islands	23.0	Madagascar	12.8
Oman	22.9	Mali	12.5
Guinea-Bissau	21.4	Chile	12.2
Burkina Faso	21.0	Algeria	12.0
Turkmenistan	19.0	United Arab Emirates	11.9
Guyana	18.5	Lao PDR	11.6
Somalia	17.8	Qatar	11.3
Suriname	17.7	Angola	11.3
Burundi	17.2	Russian Federation	10.3
Ghana	17.1		
Mongolia	16.5		
Equatorial Guinea	16.0	**Addendum**	
South Sudan	15.8	OECD members	0.5

Notes Rents are defined as the sum of oil rents, natural gas rents, coal rents (hard and soft), mineral rents, and forest rents
Source The World Bank. http://data.worldbank.org/indicator/NY.GDP.TOTL.RT.ZS, downloaded on 1 January 2018

decreasing, rather than increasing inequality, in sharp contrast to theories like the ones advocated by Frank (1966) or Wallerstein (1974).

But there are other consequences of globalization: some countries are much richer in a certain type of basic **natural resources** than others (what does not imply that they are richer in wealth or income as we will propose later on). At country-level, the World Bank is regularly publishing estimates on the relative size of such rents for more than 250 countries to assess the contribution of natural resources to economic output.[11] Table 1 merely contains the top countries surpassing the 10% line.

[11] The concept of rent here is used in the narrow definition, hence income earned due to ownership of land and the underground or above-the-ground, non-human made, natural resources (mines and forests). In other places of this book, we write about rents in a much broader sense, as incomes earned over incomes one would get on competitive markets.

The underlying explanation is straightforward. For ordinary goods and services, competitive forces expand supply until economic profits are driven to zero, but natural resources in fixed supply command returns well in excess of their cost of extraction. In countries like Liberia or Kuwait, the sum of such rents amounted to 40–50% of value "added" (GDP) in 2015.[12] Not surprisingly, this method of calculating rents shows that in the advanced OECD countries, the share of such scarcity rents is in the order of 0.5%; i.e. they are negligible. This gap between resource-rich and resource-poor countries has very important political consequences. Unfortunately, resource-based scarcity rents can even counter-balance the economic advantages of the liberal, capitalist order. Collier and Hoeffler (2009) found that thanks to their good luck of having such rents, autocracies often outperform democracies in terms of GDP growth or general well-being. According to their estimates, the critical point at which the two have equivalent effects is when resource rents (as measured by the above-shown World Bank methodology) are around 8% of GDP.

Historically though it was not always like that. The fossil fuels that powered the twentieth century were initially produced by a few, lucky countries, but a sizeable part of this rent was channeled away by oligopolistic distribution companies, like the Seven Sisters, towards the Western centers of the world economy.[13] Preceding the 1973 oil crisis, the Seven Sisters controlled around 85% of the world's petroleum reserves. Thus, through this secondary rent redistribution mechanism, cross-country inequalities actually decreased. As this important example shows globalization *per se*—i.e. internationalization of economic processes and the secondary redistribution of rents—is not so much a new phenomenon,

[12] In 2015, international oil prices were at a historical low. Three–four years earlier, the countries mentioned above earned more than 60% of their GDP in the form of rents.

[13] The Seven Sisters group which dominated the global petroleum industry from the mid-1940s to the mid-1970s consisted of: Anglo-Iranian Oil Company (now BP), Gulf Oil (later part of Chevron), Royal Dutch Shell, Standard Oil Company of California (SoCal, now Chevron), Standard Oil Company of New Jersey (Esso, later Exxon, now part of ExxonMobil), Standard Oil Company of New York (Socony, later Mobil, also now part of ExxonMobil) and Texaco (later merged into Chevron).

but as a technical term, it has, indeed, become a buzzword only not long time ago.[14]

Many of the resource-rich countries (listed in Table 1) are small and often poor—the reason being that in some of these countries (certainly not in Kuwait, or Saudi Arabia, but in Liberia, Somalia, etc.) rent-seeking is the dominant mechanism of income distribution within the country and this keeps them poor, despite their natural wealth. This is what some economists call **resource-curse** or Dutch disease.[15] But what the example of Kuwait, Saudi Arabia, or the United Arab Emirates shows—ironically all Islamic countries, hence they are supposed to be irreconcilable with the demands of a capitalist economy—resource richness in profit-oriented, well-managed countries can produce extraordinary wealth. Qatar is also such a case—often listed not far behind if not before the United Arab Emirates—as the wealthiest country on the globe. We will return to the downside of this strategy of wealth generation later.

The present-day massive flow of **migration**, supported by new and cheap means of transport/communication is primarily a consequence of globalization, but the causality works to some extent in the opposite direction, too. The policies promoting globalization incentivize people to start moving and migrating. In many rich countries, a significant part of the poor is the first or second generation of immigrants.[16] This is—partly—the consequence of the Rodrik (2013) paradox: the bottom 10% of the richest countries earn three times more than the top 10% of the poorest countries. It is highly disputed what is the total effect of migration on global inequalities. The remittances are of great and increasing importance for many poor countries and contribute to the decreasing of cross-country inequalities. They are not negligible even in

[14]The term "globalization" appeared first time with a strong emphasis in the 1994 Annual Report of the International Labor Organization (ILO) in the context of the internationalization of labor markets through outsourcing and migration. Prior to this, the term was only occasionally used by economists, see, e.g., Levitt (1983) and Smyth (1984).

[15]Dutch disease is a special form of resource-curse, when expansion of one branch industry—typically the exploitation of natural resources, such as oil hinders the development of other sectors in the country, prevents even with growing national wealth what Kornai (1972) called "harmonic growth".

[16]In 2013, the foreign-born population accounted for 13.2% of the total population in the US and 9.9% of the European Union. OECD (2015, p. 17).

post-communist countries, for instance in Poland and in Hungary with moderate, but increasing outward migration.

According to the recent estimates of the McKinsey Global Institute (2016), more than 90% of the world's 247 million cross-border migrants moved voluntarily, chiefly for economic reasons.[17] Roughly, half of them moved from developing to developed countries (though given the exceptional expansion of some developing countries, like the Gulf monarchies, China, Singapore there is a migration of skilled labor from the most developed countries to places like Saudi Arabia, Singapore or Shanghai). Workers moving to higher productivity settings boost global GDP. Migrants contributed roughly $6.7 trillion, or 9.4%, to global GDP in 2015, some $3 trillion more than they would have produced in their origin countries. North America captured up to $2.5 trillion of this augmented output, while up to $2.3 trillion went to Western Europe. Migrants of all skill levels make a positive economic contribution, whether through innovation, entrepreneurship, or freeing up natives for higher value (or for natives least desirable) work. Immigrants generally earn higher wages by moving, but many studies have found their wages remain some 20–30% below those of comparable native-born workers. Extensive academic evidence shows that immigration does not generally harm native employment or wages, although there can be short-term negative effects, if there is a large inflow of migrants into a small region, if migrants are close substitutes for native workers, or if the destination economy is experiencing a downturn from unrelated reasons (e.g. currency crisis). But is also clear, that in core countries some categories of workers were hurt by low tariffs imported from countries with cheap labor and by migrants to their own countries who were willing to offer their labor for less than natives would have done. In 2016, Donald Trump won the elections to a large extent by votes from white workers who lost jobs or had to accept lower incomes due to globalization and immigration.

An interesting **equalization mechanism** works in several Middle Eastern and Asian countries (like Hong Kong), where immigrant workers are not allowed to stay permanently—their rights are limited to the position of guest workers. The Gulf Monarchies, especially the United Arab Emirates (UAE) and Qatar are the most extreme examples

[17] The remaining 10% are refugees and asylum seekers who have fled to another country to escape conflict and persecution.

(Szelényi et al. 2018). In the UAE about 1 million from a population of 10 million are "nationals", or Emirati, hence people who are descendants of families who already lived in this area during the 1920s before the discovery of oil.[18] Thus, 90% of the population is "guest-workers", or non-nationals. The guest workers get only a visa for three years and only if they have "sponsors", local businessmen who are offering them employment. While legislation has been changing over the years and was becoming a little more liberal, these guest workers generally are not allowed to change employers. Their passport is kept by their sponsors, if they lose their jobs or for any reason they are found to be "security risks" (they violate any laws, go on strike, fight with other guest workers, etc.) they can be departed without delays by security forces. Typically, guest workers—unless they have high incomes what professionals the "West", Europe, the USA, Canada, or Australia do get—cannot bring their families to the UAE. If they please their sponsors and their job-contract is renewed, their visa can be renewed. But no matter how long they work in the UAE they have no entitlement to get citizenship, hence they do not get fringe benefits, they do not get pension and once they are unable to work they have to return "home" on some occasion to countries where they did not live for decades. The children of the very few who had high enough incomes to bring their spouses to the UAE (though they were born in Dubai or Abu Dhabi and live all their life there) cannot get citizenship and once their children reached adulthood, unless they get a job they have to return "home", to a country where they even may not speak the language.

This "exclusionary immigration regime" where only "natives" have citizenship has a lot to do with rents, generated from the oil wealth. To put it simply guest workers "do the work" especially manual and service labor (they are construction workers, waiters, taxi drivers, maids, gardeners, and also nurses, doctors, university instructors, etc.), while "natives" administer them (they are in the police, army, intelligence services, border guards, administrators in government offices). "Natives" have an extraordinary safety net, they earn high salaries, get free housing, free education and healthcare, if unemployed, generous "basic income".

[18] In principle, in the UAE only those are citizens whose family lived in one of the seven emirates before the discovery of oil. But in practice rulers (or sheikhs)—absolutist monarchs—did grant citizenship to "immigrant", especially before the UAE was established in 1971.

"Natives" live in an idealized Scandinavian welfare state, while guest workers live like people of the "third world", just with somewhat higher incomes. So, the rent coming from the scarcity of oil and OPEC smart policies serves the welfare of the small minority, the "natives".

A similar guest worker system came into being during the post-WWII years in Europe (Germany and Scandinavia). Workers came from Southern Europe and later from Turkey or from even more distant parts of the world. The USA also had a "guest worker" agreement with Mexico. The critical feature of these systems was that they only allowed people with sponsors, with visa limited to the time of their employment and they would not allow family members to join the (usually male) breadwinner already employed. The value system of liberal democracies soon questioned this inhumane arrangement, religious-ethnic discrimination against non-whites, non-Christians, though those prejudices resurface again despite the desperate need of core countries for inexpensive migrant labor to cover the costs of rents collected by "natives" from protectionism, generous welfare and pension by an aging population.

At the global worldwide scale, the combination of these two mechanisms—foreign trade and migration—lead to cross-country equalization of incomes, while the within-country inequalities rose both in the core economies and in the emerging countries as well. In other words, the two trends are inter-linked, but they change in opposite directions.

As long as the leading Western countries were growing fast and real wages were indisputably on the rise, free markets seemed to function as a positive-sum game both for firms and employees—or for capital (K) and labor (L), if we want to use the conventional notation of textbook macroeconomics. During the last 15–20 years, globalization has seemed to change brutally the outcome of the game. While statistically reported profits rose in the manufacturing branches of the US, German etc. economies, growth in real wages in the same industries were much less—if there was any growth at all. According to some specialists, this sea change is chiefly attributable to outsourcing and offshoring—i.e. the contracting out of businesses abroad. Thomas Piketty (2014) and others have concluded that this new chapter of history means a negative-sum game for low-skilled workers and employees in the developed countries.[19] Their recommendation is that something big needs to be done

[19]According to Stiglitz (2015) average hourly real earnings of production and non-supervisory employees in the US decreased some 30% between 1990 and 2009 (Part I., p. 2).

to restore the previous social balance—i.e. the previous proportions of inequalities; otherwise, the capitalist system will delegitimize itself and collapse.

Our explanation is different. For us, globalization means firstly that firms in the developed Western economies have become exposed to a more intense market competition, or using Max Weber's terminology, the previously closed social relations have become more open, and therefore much of the rents enjoyed earlier, have simply evaporated. Secondly, as the process of deindustrialization unfolded and the share of manufacturing declined in all advanced countries, it has become clear that the earlier assumption according to which industry, industrial relations and the factory model give a good approximation of the entire capitalist system, is simply untenable. The numbers of the World Bank show that the share of the manufacturing sectors' value added in American GDP is merely 12%, which is a negligible magnitude compared to the importance of the service sector (78%).[20]

Robert Solow (2015), the grand doyen of mainstream economics, has recently come to the same conclusion—although through a slightly different argumentation. This is what he wrote in a short, but very succinct paper:

> The custom is to think of value added in a corporation (or in the economy as a whole) as just the sum of the return to labor and the return to capital. But that is not quite right. There is a third component, which I will call 'monopoly rent' or, better still, just 'rent'. It is not a return earned by capital or labor, but rather a return to the special position of the firm. It may come from traditional monopoly power, being the only producer of something, but there are other ways in which firms are at least partly protected from competition. Anything that hampers competition, sometimes even regulation itself, is a source of rent. We carelessly think of it as "belonging" to the capital side of the ledger, but that is arbitrary. The division of rent among the stakeholders of a firm is something to be bargained over, formally or informally. (…) This is what has to be divided between the claimants — labor and capital and perhaps others. It is essential to understand that what we measure as wages and profits both contain an element of rent.

[20] Data refer to 2014. Source: http://data.worldbank.org/indicator/NV.IND.MANF.ZS and http://data.worldbank.org/indicator/NV.SRV.TETC.ZS, downloaded on 27 February 2017.

Solow is *not* claiming that something new happened. His main point is that rents were present in the 1950s and 1960s as well, but the majority of the profession—including Solow himself, as the author of the Solow model—disregarded them. For many decades, it *seemed* consistent with the data to assume that perfect competition prevails on the most important national markets and rents are unimportant. The two-class, closed economy,[21] manufacturing-based model appeared to fit to the data in the sense that the share of labor and capital were largely unchanged through decades in the USA, the UK and many other large and closed OECD economies.[22] With the arrival of globalization, however, **rents became suddenly visible and thus undeniable**, as third parties like the Chinese or Indian workers claimed them at the expense of shareholders and workers in the core countries.

Almost instantaneously with Solow (2015), Joseph Stiglitz (2015)—writing chiefly also about the US economy—drew the same conclusion form the newly interpreted "old" facts:

> (O)nly a slight (in the technical sense) modification of the old theories is required; but that while the modification may be technically small, this new theory has profound implications for how we view the economy, including for policy. Solow, and those working in the neoclassical tradition assumed that markets were competitive and that output was produced with labor and capital, with constant returns to scale production function. In that theory, rents played no role, because under those assumptions, there were no rents. We argue, however, that changes in rents, broadly defined (...) may be at the center of what has been happening; and that economic analysis should focus on how changes in technology - including innovations that have may have enhanced the ability of those with market power to leverage that power - institutions and policy may have increased these rents.[23]

[21] In the 1950s, the share of imports of goods and services amounted to less than 4% of GDP in the US. Today, this share is already above 15%.

[22] Nicholas Kaldor (1957) who always distanced himself from the neoclassical equilibrium models, nonetheless, took for granted the stability of the shares of GDP paid to capital and labor in the post-war period. This was one of the six most important stylized facts of growth for him. Until 2008 or so, the underlying data on US factor payments were still widely presented and interpreted in line with Kaldor's half-century-old assertion, see, e.g., Jones (2015, p. 15).

[23] Op. cit., Part I., p. 3.

The example of post-communist Eastern Europe is also a good illustration of all this. During the Cold War years, political barriers and tariffs defended the manufacturing sector in the West, because the countries of the Eastern bloc were prevented to import advanced technologies and good quality intermediate goods. *Therefore* they were incapable to produce high-quality manufactured end-products. The "white European working class" in Britain, Germany etc. enjoyed monopoly rents in addition to their wages. Take as examples the Soviet Lada or the Czechoslovak Skoda factories prior to 1989. In the absence of trade links with the West, these East European car manufacturers did not and could not pose competition to the Volkswagen or the Renault factories. Once markets were liberalized, automobile exports from Eastern Europe to Western Europe skyrocketed in the form of Eastern made Volkswagen or Renault models.

The other side of the coin is that that globalization often exposes workers in core counties to **unfair competition**. For example US textile workers now compete with semi-slave or child labor in the Philippines. In this respect, left-wing politicians of the 2016 US presidential contest such as Bernie Sanders were right to defend labor from such unfair competition. Entrepreneurs who are not bound in developing countries by fair labor laws, which limit exploitation in the core, also do collect rent. The critical question is this: to what extent globalization occurs under the same rules of market competition. Where competition is limited, rent is collected.

3 Nationalist Counterattack Against Globalization, Migration and Multi-culturalism

By definition, science is universal. Science is a search for truth and there can only be one truth. "National science" is a contradiction in terms. With culture, it is more complicated. The German term *Kultur* since the late eighteenth, the early nineteenth century is linked to the nation, it actually for some theorists constitute the nation. The English word *culture*, in contrast, is universal. It can be class specific, gender specific, race/ethnicity specific, hence multiculturalism—the coexistence and mutual cross-fertilization of various cultures which mutually respect each other—is not only possible but sensible and valuable. Since the 1960s the political right in the United States also waged "culture wars", but it was war against feminism, racial equality, anti-patriarchy and enlightenment in a way foreshadowing what recently became Alt-Right, a nostalgic dream to reconstitute WASP America, "*Make America Great Again*", what can also be interpreted as a call for restoration of old white America. But this culture war is inconsistent with the meaning of culture as it was used traditionally in the Anglo-Saxon world and it is closer to the German nationalist understanding of *Kultur*.

Anti-globalist politicians and political parties hence managed to create in some countries a broad alliance bringing on board some sections of the working class, civil servants and upper middle class promising them to keep their jobs, bring back jobs lost due to outsourcing, restore their relatively privileged incomes to pre-globalization times. Indeed while protectionist policies were pursued and migration was strictly limited or even prohibited, wage and salary earners in core countries were defended from competition from workers on the periphery of the world system. Industries, which could have been more profitably conducted in Mexico, India or China remained in the United States or Western Europe and tariffs imposed on goods produced by cheap labor in less advanced countries guaranteed higher incomes in the United States or Europe. As we defined rent in this book, workers, especially the less skilled ones collected a rent over their wages. They had incomes, which were higher than what they would have earned on competitive markets.

Anti-globalist politicians offer political packages which are often called "populist", hence they combine appeals to working class with almost left-wing social democratic policies of defending jobs and wages (bringing back jobs lost during the times a "free trade" and large-scale immigration) and a socially more broadly shared "cultural anxiety" (better term is "*Kulturangst*" as we will just refer to it). This was Donald Trump's victorious campaign strategy, calling illegal (he meant Latino) immigrants "rapists" at the first hour he announced his electoral campaign but also promising to impose tariffs—what he actually did—on products produced by cheaper labor abroad with the promise to bring manufacturing jobs back.

In a similar way, this was the strategy of Hungarian prime minister Viktor Orbán in 2015, putting large posters up all over in Hungary as refugees were approaching the Hungarian border, telling them (in the Hungarian language for Arabic speaking refugees!): "Do not take our jobs away". At the same time, the government increased incomes in the election year of 2018, while also presenting himself and the Hungarian government as a “defender of European Christian civilization”, the guarantor that Europe will not be “Islamized”. Mr. Trump’s and Mr. Orbán’s radical nationalist populism at the same time can also accommodate a policy, which makes the rich richer (see Mr. Trump’s tax reform and the flat 16% income tax introduced by the government of Mr. Orbán) and they are not particularly bothered even if their close family members, for instance their son-in-law benefit from the thus created wealth (well, they are just good businessmen…). While political power is out of their reach, the French *Front Nationale* and the German *AfD* parties use similar technics, complementing their islamophobia (and occasional anti-Semitism) with “progressive” economic policy programs. So far, they did not manage to win elections.

But let’s return to the question of culture/Kultur. Timothy Garton Ash in December 2017 published a formidable article under the title: “*It is Kultur, you stupid*” in order to explain the unexpectedly good performance of AfD in the September 2017 elections in Germany. His title is of course an ironic variation of Bill Clinton’s “*It is the economy, you stupid*” slogan. Ash presents survey data: when supporters of AfD were asked how well do they live, two third answered “well” or “very well”. Hence they are not only the “losers”, the white working class, which is attracted to AfD, but the party has a much broader appeal. Many, if not most observers (including one of the authors of this book: Iván Szelényi) were inclined to attribute Trump’s victory to the white working class, or the “counter-revolution”, the rejection of the policies of the 1960s by the white working class. Evidence for this came mainly for the surprising gain of electoral votes of Trump in the mid-Western industrial states, which usually were supposed to vote Democratic. The strong support Hillary Clinton got from college educated was seen as further proof. Such an explanation seemed to be consistent with S. M. Lipset (1960) theory of “working class authoritarianism”.

Manza and Crowley (2017) directly challenged this particular thesis. They analyzed data from the 2016 US presidential elections. They claim that what really requires explanation is not Mrs. Clinton’s loss of electoral votes in the general elections, but Trump’s nomination as Republican candidate for President. Trump defeated some of the most qualified and most experienced Republican politicians. Hence Manza and his co-author looked at results of votes cast during the nomination process. They found that Trump indeed received strong support from the white working class, but he did beat virtually all of his Republican competitors in all other major groups of white voters, including the college-educated ones. So: "It is not the working class, you stupid".

The analysis of Manza-Crowley and Ash nicely complement each other. Not that economic issues do not matter, but just economic deprivation attributed to globalization in itself does not explain the support Trump, Putin, the Polish leader Jarosław Kaczynski, Orbán, the *Jobbik*[24] *Front Nationale*, *AfD* (both of these parties follow *Jobbik*'s strategy and broaden their appeal) receives. Hence the struggle of radical national parties is as much about cultural identity and appeal to cultural anxiety (*Kulturangst*), which is shared as much by many members of the upper middle class and even some cultural and scientific intelligentsia.

It is not accidental that Ash, who writes beautiful British English, uses the German term *Kultur*, rather than the English word "culture". The reason is "culture" has more universal meaning and can be reconciled with multiculturalism, but *Kultur* is closely tied to the nation-state. "*Multikultaralism*" in German would make no sense. The same applies to the term *intelligentsia* as distinct from professionals. As Konrad and Szelényi (1979) elaborated at some length in *The Intellectuals of the Road to Class Power* four decades ago, the term *intelligentsia* was coined in Russia and referred specifically to Russian intellectuals who are not merely experts, but they represent the soul of the nation. They are not only experts of culture/civilization, they represent something deeper and more meaningful, *Kultur*. Hence there is a deep connection between the intelligentsia and the nation-state, a connection which is weak or absent among experts, professionals, who are often transnational, moving from one nation-state to the next, always move to places where their expertise can be the most efficiently applied. The Communist International (or Comintern), known also as the Third International, was exactly such an international organization of political experts—professional revolutionaries as they used the call themselves—who advocated world communism. It was founded at a Congress held in Moscow in March 1919, with the presence of 52 delegates from 34 countries.

By contrast, the intelligentsia in some nation-states today defends national *Kultur*, so it will be more receptive today to islamophobia, or outright hostile to migration especially by people who belong to another

[24]This is a Hungarian party, which is usually seen as further to the right of Mr. Orbán's party, the FIDESZ, though *Jobbik* softens its earlier xenophobic rhetoric and tries to steal the populist policies from FIDESZ.

Kultur or another race. Gil Eyal (2003) in his insightful book on the causes of the breakup of Czechoslovakia, inspired by *The Intellectuals on the Road to Class Power* demonstrated that Slovak independence was strongly supported by Slovak intelligentsia. For them, it was in their best interest to sharpen the differences between Czech and Slovak language and gain monopoly over Slovak cultural and even governmental institutions.

The term intelligentsia is largely absent in Anglo-Saxon, especially in the American culture. What comes the closest in the American discourse to the concept of intelligentsia is the term "public intellectuals". Public intellectuals do not lock themselves into their professional ghettos (like academic departments at universities and their professional association); they want to reach out to the broader public, to publish op-ed pieces in the *New York Times*, write for *New York Review of Books* and try to avoid the peer-reviewed professional journals. Also inspired by *The Intellectuals on the Road to Class Power*, Eleanor Townsley wrote a fine book in this spirit on *New York Intellectuals* (2009).

In order to preserve rent secured to domestic workers and *Kultur*-specialists migration is a major challenge. It has to be limited to those who are likely to be able to assimilate to national *Kultur* (hence people with different but strong culture, religion, different skin color are looked upon with suspicion).

References

Collier, P., and A. Hoeffler. 2009. Testing the Neo-Con Agenda: Democracy in Resource-Rich Societies. *European Economic Review* 53: 293–308.

Eyal, Gil. 2003. *The Origins of Postcommunist Elites: From the Prague Spring to the Breakup of Czechoslovakia*. Minneapolis: University of Minnesota Press.

Frank, André Gunder. 1966. *The Development and Underdevelopment*. New York: Monthly Review Press.

Jones, Charles I. 2015. The Facts of Economic Growth. NBER Working Paper Series, 21142, May.

Kaldor, Nicholas. 1957. A Model of Economic Growth. *The Economic Journal* 67 (268): 591–624.

Kornai, János. 1972. *Rush Versus Harmonic Growth: Meditation on the Theory and on the Policies of Economic Growth*. Amsterdam and London: North-Holland Publishing.

Kornai, János. 2016. So What Is Capital in the Twenty-First Century? Some Notes on Piketty's Book. *Capitalism & Society* 11 (1).

Konrád, György, and Iván Szelényi. 1979. *Intellectuals on the Road to Class Power*. New York: Harcourt, Brace and Jovanovich.

Lenin, V.I. [1916] 2010. *Imperialism, the Highest Stage of Capitalism*. London: Penguin.

Levitt, Theodore. 1983. Globalization of Markets. *Harvard Business Review*, May–June.

Lewis, William. 2004. *The Power of Productivity: Wealth, Poverty, and the Threat to Global Stability*. Chicago: The University of Chicago Press.

Lipset, Seymour Martin. [1960] 1981. *Political Man*. Baltimore: Johns Hopkins University Press.

Manza, Jeff, and Ned Crowley. 2017. Working Class Hero? Interrogation the Social Base of the Rise of Donald Trump. *The Forum* 15 (1): 3–28.

McKinsey Global Institute (MGI). 2016. *People on the Move: Global Migration's Impact and Opportunity*. MGI.

OECD. 2015. *In It Together, Why Less Inequality Benefits All*. Paris: OECD Publishing. https://doi.org/10.1787/9789264235120-en.

Piketty, Thomas. 2014. *Capital in the Twenty-First Century*. Cambridge: Harvard University Press.

Rodrik, Dani. 2013. The Past, Present, and Future of Economic Convergence. http://www.sss.ias.edu/files/pdfs/Rodrik/Presentations/Past-Present-and-Future-Economic-Convergence-(October2013).pdf.

Smyth, Don. 1984. Achievements, New Directions from 1994 ILO conference, *Monthly Labor Review*, September.

Solow, Robert. 2015. The Future of Work, Why Wages Aren't Keeping Up? *Pacific Standard*, August 11.

Stiglitz, Joseph. 2002. *Globalization and Its Discontents*. New York: W.W. Norton.

Stiglitz, Joseph. 2015. New Theoretical Perspectives on the Distribution of Income and Wealth Among Individuals, Parts I–IV. NBER Working Paper Series, 21189, 21190, 21191, 21192.

Szelényi, Iván (in collaboration with Riaz Hassan and Vladislav Maksimov). 2018. *Building Nations with Non-nationals: The Exclusionary Immigration Regimes of the Gulf Monarchies with a Case study of Pakistani Return Migrants from and Prospective Migrants to the United Arab Emirates*. Budapest: Corvina.

Townsley, Eleanor. 2009. *The Sociology of Intellectual Life: The Career of the Mind in and Around Academy*. London: Sage.

Wallerstein, Immanuel. 1974. *The Modern World System*. New York: Academic Press.

CHAPTER 7

Theoretical and Policy Conclusions

Abstract What is unfolding in front of our eyes is the greatest emancipatory achievement of humankind since the Enlightenment. The danger is, however, that countries predominantly and lastingly based on rent-seeking tend to be economically stagnating or declining and socially unstable. The purpose of this book was not to make a case *against* rent-seeking and *for* profit-seeking. Pareto's observation seems to be insightful still today: a modern market economy needs both speculators and rentiers: foxes and lions. But too many foxes, too much speculation, too much unrestrained markets can cause instability, The lowest possible VAT and modest taxes on wages and profits compensated by as high tax rates on inheritance and capital gain taxes as practically possible, seem to serve both social justice and economic dynamism.

Keywords Cross-country equalization of incomes · Rising within-country inequalities · Speculation · Rentiers · Wealth tax · Inheritance tax · VAT

This last chapter briefly summarizes our theoretical and policy lessons.

P. Mihályi and I. Szelényi,
Rent-Seekers, Profits, Wages and Inequality,
https://doi.org/10.1007/978-3-030-03846-5_7

1 Theoretical Conclusions

The main theoretical ambition of the book is to change the discourse about inequality. What matters is not the extent of inequality, but its source. Inequality becomes a major social (and economic issue) if it is driven by rent. **Rent-generated inequalities** undermine the meritocratic legitimacy of liberal capitalism and the efficiency of capital investments. We distinguished 13 types of rents (see Table 1 in Chapter 3) derived from two main categories of rents: scarcity rents and solidarity rents. Many of them are functioning as intrinsic building blocks of all enlightened, liberal market economies. Rents and rent-seeking cannot and should not be eliminated from our system. The discourse about inequality focused during the past few years on the top 1.0 or top 0.1%. This, in our view, is misleading. On the very top of income, social mobility tends to be high and it is less of a political concern. But there is not only a growing gap between the top 10–20% versus the rest but given the inheritance of wealth, that wealth is perceived as "unearned". Piketty is correct: society tends to become more "patrimonial". On the top, privileges are more likely to pass over to the next generation.

Let's elaborate.

A. As we argued in this before there is only a loose correlation between economic inequality on the one hand and economic growth or social stability on the other. Countries with high GINI achieved occasionally dynamic economic growth (that is true from most of the history of the United States to most of post-Maoist China) and high-income inequalities. As long as those incomes are perceived as "earned" they could be accepted socially. In the nineteenth- and most of the twentieth-century United States and post-Maoist China as long as people believed in the "American" or in the "Chinese" dream—namely that if we work hard we can all achieve great affluence—inequality was not challenged. On the other hand, some of the history's most prosperous countries like Scandinavia from the 1930s until the late decades of the twentieth century functioned very well with low GINI coefficients. They produced dynamic economic development as well, plus they created unprecedented social peace and harmony, too. High earners were willing to accept high taxes, as long as they believed that their democratically elected government would spend their taxes in economically productive and socially just ways (e.g. spending it on cleaning the air and water, building highways, high-speed trains, public transportation and helping the needy with proper education, healthcare, pension system, and public housing). And as long as it was believed that tax revenues were not used to provide rents to state clients and public funds were not used to secure longer tenure for the ruling political parties in government, there were no tax-revolts.

Hence the main conclusion of this book is: the extent of inequality per se is not the problem. The question is how much of inequalities in income and wealth are stemming from wages and profits earned on competitive markets and how much inequality is created by rents generated by the restriction of market competition. **Societies predominantly based on rent-seeking tend to be economically stagnating or declining and socially unstable**, while economies based on free market competition tend to be economically dynamic and socially reasonably stable.

B. Let's try to simplify the types of rents as much as possible just to make the key points of this book as clear as we can. The 13 types we described in Chapter 3 can be classified into two broader categories: scarcity rents (this is the concept D. Ricardo introduced in the mid-nineteenth century) and solidarity rents (which is our addition to the literature). The first one is income gained from restrictions of market competition, the second from either corrections of market failures or attempts to improve market competition. The second one includes social redistribution (such as social welfare) or it includes public interventions to improve competitiveness (for instance by government funding of basic research, creating better public education, various forms of affirmative action for ethnic minorities, migrants, or women).

Scarcity rents can stem either from the normal functioning of the markets or by the intervention of governmental or other public bodies. As we learned from Polanyi or Schumpeter—just to name two major twentieth-century authors markets can be self destructive. Remember Schumpeter's famous verdict: can capitalism survive? No. But not because it is not sufficiently successful, but because it is too successful…. Uncontrolled markets can limit competition in more than one way. One or a few firms may just "over-accumulate", hence to make entry of new firms with insufficient capital into the market impossible or very difficult even if they could be more efficient and more profitable than the existing large corporations. Some large firms can even attain a monopoly situation. This happened to the Ford empire during the late nineteenth century (which in part was achieved not just by capturing the whole market horizontally and vertically through rootless competition, but was also helped by paying government officials to pass legislation in their favor and using coercive methods, even murdering competitors: "one drop of oil is one drop of blood"). More often large firms form oligopolies or cartels, hence several market-dominating firms reach a price setting agreement with each other (OPEC being a clear example). Monopolies, oligopolies, cartels beyond earning a profit also collect a "rent"; hence they have an income higher than what they would have had on a competitive market. (True, Richard Posner (1975) was right: making a monopoly, an oligopoly or a cartel has also "costs", so to achieve such status firms have to invest, and some of their income may be profit earned on this investment.) Our key point is however that monopolies, oligopolies, cartels beyond earning profit do generate a rent, hence an "unearned" income, which comes from the fact they excluded competition for the services or products they offer.

We see globalization as an important, praiseworthy new stage of the world economy. At the global scale, the combination of fast-growing foreign trade, the international movement of capital and labor (migration) leads to *cross-country equalization of incomes*, while the within-country inequalities rose both in the core economies and in the emerging countries. In other words, the two trends are inter-linked, but they change in opposite directions. What is unfolding in front of our eyes is arguably *the greatest emancipatory achievement of humankind since the Enlightenment.* Tens of millions of people are on the road escaping wars, natural disasters, and poverty. Many more are economic migrants; their only aim is to create humanly acceptable conditions for themselves and their families. Is that a crime? Was the extraordinary growth of countries like the United States and Canada not driven by "economic migrants" from Ireland, Italy, and Eastern Europe? But we do see that globalization while advancing free competition is also a source of rent-generation for multi-national firms. Globalization destroys some (occasionally high quality) local companies and local working places, but it is an empirical question to what extent—for global social justice—this needs to be compensated.

In pre-capitalist societies—in particular, in the system called feudal—, typical income was rent. While there were profit-seeking or wage-earning individuals even in ancient Rome, India, or China but since the feudal economies were not market integrated, profits and wages were the exceptions, and rent was *the* rule of the game. Ruler gave estates and secured this way rental incomes to the lords he trusted, or whose support he anticipated in the future. And the same logic applied through the whole social hierarchy. Landowning nobility allowed serfs/peasants to cultivate a piece of land and offered them protection in exchange for specific services and loyalty.

Capitalist market economies are driven primarily by profit-seeking and wage-maximizing logics. Scarcity rents if they are the results of intervention by governments and public bodies into the functioning of markets are usually defined as corruption. The most obvious example is when political actors interfere with free competition and give priority or at least advantages in market competition to their clients in order to buy or reward their loyalty. This will be defined as corruption especially if the client is suspected to be a "Strohman", who is collecting (at least some of the) wealth for the political boss. Such rent-seeking practices are spotted in many African and other developing countries, but some evidence of rent-seeking can be spotted in *all* capitalist economies. Liberal critiques of President Trump often suspect that in his administration political power is used to generate incomes, and some of such incomes may go to the president himself, to his daughter, or son-in-law.

In this book, we devoted special attention to the corruption in post-communist economies. We are certainly not the first to spot this tendency; Klebnikov already in 2001 wrote about Yeltsin as the "godfather of the Kremlin", Magyar (2016) labeled the post-2010 Hungarian regime as "mafia state". Our novel contribution is that we focus on rent-seeking behavior. While this focus is politically more subdued and intends to be analytical rather than ethical/political, by drawing the attention to the dangers of the process in which profit-seeking is substituted by rent-seeking, we intend to draw attention to the long-term risks of post-communist economies which is not just some policy error of individual governments, but an (avoidable, but nevertheless) inherent tendency in post communism. Nevertheless, a final word of warning about the uses of the term "corruption" is warranted. Anti-corruption campaigns are *en vogue* all over the world, especially in authoritarian regimes, or regimes which tend to move in the authoritarian direction. Putin and Xi, Erdogan and Orbán (many similar examples can be found in Latin America, Asia, Africa) are all "fighting corruption" (though by their opposition they themselves are suspected to be corrupt). There seems to be ample evidence that these anti-corruption campaigns are often used as tools to fight political enemies. People are not jailed, because they would be a threat if they would compete in the electoral campaign or because they have "dissenting views", but they are disgraced since they are accused to cheat on their taxes or to handle public money in irresponsible ways.

When we explore the composition of incomes which take the form of wages the case is not much simpler either. Governments and public bodies intervene in the supply of labor with various qualifications. One often needs a specific license to practice a particular occupation, and issuing such permits gives the authority to governmental or other public bodies the power to control the supply of specific skills (medical doctors of legal practitioners are prime examples). Selective admission of elite schools—and higher rewards to degrees earned in such schools—also create rent, a component of the income people with such education will attain. As Grusky and Sorensen (1998) pointed it out trade unions also added—while they were powerful—rent to the wages of ordinary workers. The disintegration of trade unions is in part of the decline of wages/incomes in the core countries of the world economy.

As far as solidarity rents are concerned, we are faced with a similar dilemma, as in the case of scarcity rents. Solidarity rent usually also has a component of competition-based earnings. For instance, rent for innovation or rent based on licenses push the earnings of innovators over what they would earn on free markets. This is a kind of pre-payment in anticipation of high competitive performance—thus a contribution to public welfare—at a later point in time. Rents paid for the poor (in terms of social welfare, pensions, free Medicare, or in affirmative action) are also unearned, but in part, they can be acknowledgments of past or anticipated future productivity. Let us also add, while solidarity rent is usually seen as the opposite of corruption, those who claim that taxes are too high and government expenditures on welfare or affirmative action are too big, are also inclined to see these compensating policies as "corrupt". There is no single "objective" criterion how to find what corruption is. It is a politically contested concept, and we conclude: at the systemic level, **the critical question is when profit-seeking behavior is significantly overruled by the logic of the rent-seeking economy**.

In sum, it is hard to tell, where can draw the line between rent collectors and those who collect income earned as profit or wages/salaries on competitive markets. Most of those who collect profits also earn rent, many whose income is from wages and salaries may have some rental income. One of the most important contributions of this book to the theory of inequality is that **incomes of capital owners, but also of the skilled and less skilled workers come in part from rents**. Such a division of incomes between wages vs. profits on the one hand and rents on the other is theoretically very important, though empirically it is tough to be estimated.

C. In this book, we challenge the received wisdom that in the advanced Western democracies the critical social closure is between the top 1 or even 0.1% of the society and the rest. While it is indeed true that the most extraordinary growth of income and wealth can be seen in the top 1 or less than 1%, we suggest that the essential closure from the rest of society is much further below that level. We would draw that line where "relative mobility" has been reduced during the past few decades. In the top of the social hierarchy, a new "aristocracy" or "estate" is being created. The likelihood to enter such positions is reduced; the likelihood that those who were born in the highest group will fall into lower strata is limited. Our principal assertion is that **the dividing line is around the top 20%**. Whether it is just the 20 or 10 or whatever percent may vary from time to time from country to country. We do not claim we know where the real cut-off point is, but this book is an invitation for further research on a country-by-country or epoch-by-epoch bases.

2 Policy Conclusions

So what is to be done, what are the policy implications—if any? We do not believe in a "single tax" system. For us Ricardo's preferred solution is only a point of departure. Partly because Ricardo uses—in comparison with Sorensen—a narrow definition of rent. Rent for him was ground rent. But in Chapter X of his *Principles of Political Economy and Taxation*, he makes a compelling argument—one which we want to generalize for the broader concept of rent: "A tax on rent would affect rent only: it would fall wholly on landlords, and could not be shifted to any class of consumers".[1] In the most radical formulation that means that taxes on rents is the only tax, which does not have an inflationary effect, taxing profits and wages/salaries do have such an impact.

[1] Ricardo ([1817] 2004, p. 110).

But even Ricardo's narrower definition of land—as ground rent—faces challenges. Rents paid even to the landlords have a "profit component" (this is our interpretation, not Ricardo's terminology). The payment the tenant has to pay to the landlord for the uses of the land he/she cultivates also does not merely represent an "unearned income" by the monopolistic owner of the land, but he/she also has to recover the improvements on the land the landlord created. Those improvements (building roads, improving the productivity of land, creation of buildings, fences, etc.) or "profit investment", improve productivity hence taxing them would have an inflationary effect.

Now let's return—a la Sorensen—to our broader conception of rent. Tax on income (be it from wages or profit) tends to have an inflationary effect, tax on rent (unearned incomes) does not. But before we elaborate, let us make it clear at the outset: "Tax the 1 percent" is populist demagoguery. There is no way how one can generate enough public income just taxing the wealthiest 1% and in addition, the wealthiest 1% may make socially productive investments and we may not want to discourage such investments. In order to simplify our recommendation as much as we can: the fairest tax system is a tax on inheritance and capital gain.

Unfortunately, even this is not as simple as it appears. Theoretically, the socially fairest and economically the most effective system of taxation to put it in the most general way is **a tax on unearned income**. But there are many limitations to implementing this. Let's begin with the conservative critique of inheritance tax, as "death tax". This is a reasonable argument. After all inheritance tax is "double taxation", assets which are inherited were initially taxed so why do we tax them at the second time? The most important argument for inheritance tax is that in this case we do not tax the one who created those assets (and paid taxes for it), but those who receive it "unearned". Their parents paid the taxes, not they. Besides the assets they inherit tend to be much higher capital value than the assets initially invested, so taxing capital gains seems to be socially just and economically rational. Furthermore, as it is obvious from the above argument, some compensation paid as "rent" has a profit component and all income which appears to be profits or wages may have a "rent" component. Empirically it is almost impossible to distinguish which part of income is actually rent, profit, or wage. That will justify levying taxes on exceptionally high profits of wages as well, since we have good reason to believe that some of it is "unearned".

There are also practical reasons why imposing too high taxes on inheritance and taxing profits and wages—to some extent—may have their limits. If inheritance tax is close to 100% it indeed may create disincentives to savings ("If the state will pocket my wealth when I die and not my family, why should I save?"), though high levels of savings within the national economies are essential for their healthy economic growth. It is also hard to enforce a too high inheritance tax (or for that sake any excessive tax rate—be it on wages or profits). Owners of large wealth will find legal loopholes to rescue their wealth from inheritance taxes, by creating trust funds; begin to buy a new property in the name of their children or wife etc. Denmark used to impose one of the world's highest marginal tax rates on wealth at the top of the distribution, but this tax was drastically reduced and ultimately abolished between 1989 and 1997.[2] The case of Japan is also educative. The 55% marginal rate of the inheritance tax was initially meant for Japanese citizens living in Japan. Then some of the very rich moved out (on paper) from Japan to avoid this tax, which in turn incentivized law-makers to extend the scope of the tax to Japanese citizens living outside of Japan and it was calculated on all assets wherever they could be found on earth. Once this was done, the problem arose that foreign investors were actively discouraged to move into Japan, because in this case, the 55% marginal rate would apply their properties located in other places than Japan. Now, Japan is also considering doing something about this uncertain situation.[3] The same is true for taxes on profits or wages. If those taxes are too high, entrepreneurs or highly paid wage earners may move to "tax havens".

We are not alone with our proposition emphasizing the importance of inheritance tax. It is noteworthy that the world's wealthiest self-made people, such as Warren Buffet and Bill Gates advocate voluntary wealth-transfers. In 2010, at their initiative, 40 of America's wealthiest individuals and couples joined together in a commitment to give more than half of their wealth away during their lifetime. As of May 2018, there are 183 pledgers from 22 countries[4] setting a new standard of generosity among the ultra-wealthy.

[2] Jakobsen et al. (2017).

[3] https://www.bloomberg.com/news/articles/2017-11-12/tokyo-pushes-back-on-bizarre-death-tax-that-deters-expats.

[4] https://givingpledge.org/About.aspx, accessed on 6 August 2018.

Our concluding policy conclusions: not having inheritance tax is socially not just and economically not rational. But for practical purposes some degree of inheritance tax in combination for the—assumed—rent component of profits and wages/salaries is also sensible and justified.

3 Final Comments

Klebnikov (2001) compared the Russian oligarchs to the American Robber Barons of the late nineteenth century. They had lots in common. But, as Klebnikov pointed out, the Robber Barons produced something and contributed to economic growth in the United States, by operating (a quite) large island of a competitive market economy. From the benefit of hindsight, many scholars of the post-communist economies agree that the Russian oligarchs did not produce much or anything, but deposited their incomes gained just from rent in Swiss banks and accumulated spectacular wealth in real estate on the Riviera, in London or in Florida, not speaking of their yachts and art collections. In the early parts of the 1990s, this was not yet clear. Aslund (1999) and others justified their activities by claiming that the brutal behavior of the oligarchs was needed to overcome the resistance of the old *nomenklatura*. As of today, it seems that President Putin captured the oligarchs—as we analyzed above—, but he also reversed the positive market reforms of the 1990s.[5]

The purpose of this book was not to make a case *against* rent-seeking and *for* profit-seeking. Pareto's observation (1916) seems to be insightful still today: a modern market economy needs both speculators and rentiers: foxes and lions. The complex eco-system of market capitalism needs both animals. Too many foxes, too much speculation, too much unrestrained markets can cause instability and it may require what Polanyi in *The Great Transformation* called the "double movement". It may require a transformation of some of the market earned profits or wages into rent to those who cannot provide for themselves on the market (that is what welfare redistribution is). But too many lions, too much rent-seeking can suffocate competition. Let's cite one more time John Locke (1698):

[5] As Aslund himself formulated in a recent article: "Putin's regime has degraded the institutions that are essential to the functioning of a modern economy. The judicial system, for example, is largely in tatters. And above all, the ownership and governance of key assets and resources are almost all in state hands." Aslund and Commander (2016). See also Aslund (2013).

"This is to think that Men are so foolish that they take care to avoid what Mischiefs may be done them by Pole-cats, or foxes, but are content, may think it Safety, to be devoured by lions".[6] Of course Locke here means fellow citizen competitors as foxes and the absolute monarch as the lion, but let's translate this into the language of Pareto and we get to the bottom line of our book: Foxes are fellow competitors, who may outsmart us, lions are rentiers who already outsmarted us, by (ab)using their political connections to restrict competition to their advantage.

Finally, when discussing inequalities, it is a mistake to focus on the wealth of the top 1.0% or 0.1%, as Piketty does, because the positions in these elite groups are not long-lasting and not necessarily hereditary. Through the combined effect of accumulated human and social capital, higher per capita incomes, inherited real estates and assortative mating, the yawning gap between the families of the top 20% and the rest of the society is much more upsetting. There is a great deal of irony in the fact, that the enthusiastic supporters of Piketty's book, who likely belong to the patrimonial upper class, the top 20% of their own countries everywhere, are so irritated by the wealth of the top 1%. As Robert Solow maliciously noted, there is a relationship between this biased focus of the Piketty book and its phenomenal international success: envy is a more powerful emotion than compassion.[7] In our view, the increasingly privileged position of the upper middle class poses a grave danger to open society and the excessive attention paid to the top 1% distracts attention from this and serves the interest of this class.

Our main inference is that the crucial question is not the extent of measured inequality (income or wealth). Countries with Gini around 0.20 or 0.40 can equally be economically dynamic and socially cohesive. Beyond the ethno-racial, religious, and gender-based social gaps, the key question is: are inequalities stemming from a mechanism, which generates competition as free as one conceivably can create between workers vs. workers, capitalists vs. capitalists or it arises from rent-seeking, hence the exclusion of some players from the competition by the politically connected ones. While we would not go as far as Sorensen and assume an "antagonistic", class division between rent collectors vs. those whose

[6]Op. cit., p. 328.

[7]Robert Solow in Conversation with Paul Krugman: "Inequality: What Can Be Done?", 1 May 2015, https://www.youtube.com/watch?v=DGmUtJkTaqc.

income stems from profit or wages, we share Ricardo's position, namely, that it is sensible to tax rents rather than profits and wages. The current tax rates on property/wealth are astonishingly low in all of the OECD countries at the macroeconomic level, and *therefore* the present situation allows a considerable maneuvering room for future change.

The economic space is there. In 2015, the combined revenue from all kind of estate, inheritance and gif taxes as a percentage of GDP was merely 0.1% in the OECD countries (Belgium and France having the highest rates, 0.7 and 0.6%, respectively).[8] By contrast, in the post-communist countries, where the first generation of successful entrepreneurs is about to retire and/or pass away the inheritance tax was recently abolished—a change into the undesirable direction.[9] The economically and socially most problematic form of taxation is VAT. High level of VAT tends to burden the poorest of the poor (and in fact—much like inheritance tax—is also double taxation).

The other frequently used argument, namely that low wealth-transfer taxes encourage more work and more savings is logical but lacks statistical evidence. Considering all other options of revenue collections, the lowest possible VAT and modest taxes on wages and profits compensated by as high tax rates on inheritance and capital gain taxes as practically possible seem to serve both social justice and economic dynamism.

References

Aslund, Anders. 1999. *How Russia Became a Market Economy*. Washington, DC: The Brookings Institution.

Aslund, Anders. 2013. Russia Can't Grow and Steal at the Same Time. *Moscow Times*, November 27.

Aslund, Anders, and Simon Commander. 2016. Russia's Gloomy Prospects. *Project Syndicate*, May 9.

Grusky, David, and Jesper B. Sørensen. 1998. Can Class Analysis Be Salvaged? *American Journal of Sociology* 103: 1187–1234.

[8] https://stats.oecd.org/Index.aspx?DataSetCode=REV, accessed 6 August 2018.

[9] In Hungary, for example, inherited property is exempt from inheritance tax, if the property inherited by the testator's parent or child or spouse since 2010. The same hold for financial assets, like savings accounts, equity or bonds.

Jakobsen, Katrine, Kristian Jakobsen, Henrik Kleven, and Gabriel Zucman. 2017. Wealth Taxation and Wealth Inequality: Evidence from Denmark, 1980–2014. Manuscript. https://editorialexpress.com/cgi-bin/conference/download.cgi?db_name=NTA2017&paper_id=315.

Klebnikov, P. 2001. *Godfather of the Kremlin*. New York: Houghton Mifflin Harcourt.

Locke, John. [1698] 1988. *Two Treatise of Government*. Cambridge: Cambridge University Press.

Magyar, Bálint. 2016. *Post-Communist Mafia State*. Budapest: Central European University Press.

Pareto, Vilfredo. [1916] 1935. *The Mind and Society* (Trattato Di Sociologia General). New York: Harcourt, Brace.

Posner, Richard A. 1975. The Social Costs on Monopoly and Regulation. *The Journal of Political Economy* 4: 807–828.

Ricardo, David. [1817] 2004. *Principles of Political Economy and Taxation*. Mineola, NY: Dover Publications.

Bibliography

Acemoglu, D., and J. Robinson. 2012. *Why Nations Fail: The Origins of Power, Prosperity, and Poverty*. Boston: Harvard University Press.

Aghion, Philippe, Ufuk Akcigit, Antonin Bergeaud, Richard William Blundell, and David Hemous. 2015. Innovation and Top Income Inequality. CEPR Discussion Paper No. 10659.

Akerlof, George, and Robert Shiller. 2015. *Phishing for Phools: The Economics of Manipulation and Deception*. Princeton: Princeton University Press.

Andrews, Dan, Chiara Criscuolo, and Peter N. Gal. 2015. Frontier Firms, Technology Diffusion and Public Policy: Micro Evidence from OECD Countries. The Future of Productivity: Main Background Papers. Paris: OECD.

Ash, Timothy Garton. 2017. It's the Kultur, Stupid. *The New York Review of Books*, December 7.

Aslund, Anders. 1999. *How Russia Became a Market Economy*. Washington, DC: The Brookings Institution.

Aslund, Anders. 2013. Russia Can't Grow and Steal at the Same Time. *Moscow Times*, November 27.

Aslund, Anders, and Simon Commander. 2016. Russia's Gloomy Prospects. *Project Syndicate*, May 9.

Atkinson, Anthony. 2015. *Inequality: What Can Be Done?* Cambridge: Harvard University Press.

Attanasio, Orazio P., and Luigi Pistaferri. 2016. Consumption Inequality. *Journal of Economic Perspectives* 30 (2): 3–28.

P. Mihályi and I. Szelényi,
Rent-Seekers, Profits, Wages and Inequality,
https://doi.org/10.1007/978-3-030-03846-5

Autor, David, David Dorn, F. Lawrence Katz, Christina Patterson, and John Van Reenen. 2017. The Fall of the Labor Share and the Rise of Superstar Firms. NBER Working Paper No. 23396, May.

Balestra, Carlotta, and Richard Tonkin. 2018. Inequalities in Household Wealth Across OECD Countries: Evidence from the OECD Wealth Distribution Database. OECD Statistics and Data Directorate Working Paper No. 88, 20 June.

Bhagwati, Jagdish N. 1982. Directly Unproductive Profit-Seeking (DUP) Activities. *Journal of Political Economy* 90: 988–1002.

Bohle, Dorothee, and Béla Greskovits. 2012. *Capitalist Diversity on Europe's Periphery*. Ithaca and London: Cornell University Press.

Bourdieu, P., and J.-C. Passeron. [1970] 1977. *Reproduction in Education, Society and Culture*. London: Sage.

Buchanan, J. M., R.D. Tollison, and Gordon Tullock (eds.). 1980. *Toward a Theory of Rent Seeking Society*. College Station: Texas A&M University Press.

Burawoy, Michael. 1984. Karl Marx and the Satanic Mills: Factory Politics Under Early Capitalism in England and the United States. *American Journal of Sociology* 90 (2): 247–282.

Clark, G. 2014. *The Son Also Rises*. Princeton: Princeton University Press.

Collier, P., and A. Hoeffler. 2009. Testing the Neo-Con Agenda: Democracy in Resource-Rich Societies. *European Economic Review* 53: 293–308.

Congleton, Roger D., Arye L. Hillman, and Kai A. Konrad. 2008. *40 Years of Research on Rent Seeking*, Vols. 1 and 2. Berlin: Spinger.

Conley, Dalton. 1999. *Being Black and Living in Red*. Berkeley: University of California Press.

Csillag, Tamas, and Iván Szelényi. 2015. Drifting from Liberal Democracy. *Intersection* 1 (1): 1–31.

Darvas, Zsolt. 2016. Some Are More Equal Than Others: New Estimates of Global and Regional Inequality. Bruegel Working Papers, Issue 8.

Deaton, Angus. 2013. *The Great Escape: Health, Wealth, and the Origins of Inequality*. Princeton: Princeton University Press.

Engels, Jens Ivo. 2014. *Die Geschichte der Korruption: Von der Frühen Neuzeit bis ins 20. Jahrhundert* [The History of Corruption: From the Early Modern Period to the 20th Century]. Frankfurt am Main: Fischer.

Eyal, Gil. 2003. *The Origins of Postcommunist Elites: From the Prague Spring to the Breakup of Czechoslovakia*. Minneapolis: University of Minnesota Press.

Eyal, Gil., Iván Szelényi, and E. Townsley. 1998. *Making Capitalism Without Capitalists*. London: Verso.

Felipe, Jesus, and John S.L. McCombie. 2013. *The Aggregate Production Function and the Measurement of Technical Change: 'Not Even Wrong'*. Cheltenham: Edwar Elgar.

Filmer, Robert. [1680] 2017. *Patriarcha, or the Natural Power of Kings*. New York: Routledge.

Folsom, Burton W. [1987] 2010. *The Myth of the Robber Barons.* Herndon, VA: Young America's Foundation.

Frank, André Gunder. 1966. *The Development and Underdevelopment.* New York: Monthly Review Press.

Fuest, Clemens, Florian Neumeier, and Daniel Stöhlker. 2018. Why the IMS and OECD Are Wrong About Inequality and Growth. *EconPol Policy Brief* 2, May.

Furman, Jason, and Peter Orszag. 2015. A Firm-Level Perspective on the Role of Rents in the Rise in Inequality. Presentation at "A Just Society" Centennial Event in Honor of Joseph Stiglitz Columbia University, 16 October. Manuscript.

George, Henry. [1879] 1886. *Progress and Poverty.* London: Kegan Paul, Trench.

Gimpelson, Vladimir, and Daniel Treisman. 2015. Misperceiving Inequality. NBER Working Papers No. 21174.

Grusky, David, and Jesper B. Sørensen. 1998. Can Class Analysis Be Salvaged? *American Journal of Sociology* 103: 1187–1234.

Guerriero, Marta. 2012. The Labor Share of Income Around the World: Evidence from a Panel Dataset. University of Manchester, Institute for Development Policy and Management, Working Paper No. 32.

Hankiss, Elemér. 1990. *East European Alternatives.* Oxford: Clarendon Press.

Hayek, F.A. 1979. *Law, Legislation and Liberty: The Political Order of the Free People.* Chicago: University of Chicago Press.

Henderson, Bruce. 1976. The Rule of Three and Four, ld. https://www.bcgperspectives.com/content/Classics/strategy_the_rule_of_three_and_four/.

Huang, P. 2011. Chongqing: Equitable Development Driven by a 'Third Hand'? *Modern China* 6: 559–622.

International Labour Office. 2017. *Global Estimates of Child Labour: Results and Trends, 2012–2016.* Geneva.

Jackson, Michelle, and David Grusky. 2018. A Cultural Theory of Structural Loss. *British Journal of Sociology (forthcoming).*

Jacobs, Didier. 2015. Extreme Wealth Is Not Merited. Oxfam Discussion Papers, November.

Jakobsen, Katrine, Kristian Jakobsen, Henrik Kleven, and Gabriel Zucman. 2017. Wealth Taxation and Wealth Inequality: Evidence from Denmark, 1980–2014. Manuscript. https://editorialexpress.com/cgi-bin/conference/download.cgi?db_name=NTA2017&paper_id=315.

Jones, Charles I. 2015. The Facts of Economic Growth. NBER Working Paper Series, 21142, May.

Josephson, M. 1934. *The Robber Barons.* New York: Harcourt.

Kaldor, Nicholas. 1957. A Model of Economic Growth. *The Economic Journal* 67 (268): 591–624.

Kaldor, Nicholas. [1934a] 1960: A Classificatory Note on the Determinateness of Equilibrium. In *Essays on Value and Distribution*, 13–33. London: Duckworth.

Kaldor, Nicholas. [1934b] 1960. The Equilibrium of the Firm. In *Essays on Value and Distribution*, 34–50. London: Duckworth.

Kaldor, Nicholas. [1935] 1960. Market Imperfection and Excess Capacity. In *Essays on Value and Distribution*, 62–80. London: Duckworth.

Kaldor, Nicholas. [1938] 1960. Professor Chamberlin on Monopolistic and Imperfect Competition. In *Essays on Value and Distribution*, 81–95. London: Duckworth.

Keen, Steve. 2011. *Debunking Economics—Revised and Expanded Edition*. London and New York: Zed Books.

Keynes, J. Maynard. [1920] 1971. *The Economic Consequences of the Peace*. New York: Harper Torchbooks.

Khan, Shamus Rahman. 2011. *Privilege: The Making of an Adolescent Elite at St. Saul's High School*. Princeton: Princeton University Press.

King, L., and Iván Szelényi. 2005. Post-communist Economic Systems. In *The Handbook of Economic Sociology*, ed. S. Neil and R. Swedberg, 206–232. Princeton: Princeton University Press.

Klebnikov, P. 2001. *Godfather of the Kremlin*. New York: Houghton Mifflin Harcourt.

Kolosi, Tamás, and Iván Szelényi. 2010. *Hogyan legyünk milliárdosok?* Budapest: Corvina (in Hungarian).

Konrád, György, and Iván Szelényi. 1979. *Intellectuals on the Road to Class Power*. New York: Harcourt, Brace and Jovanovich.

Kornai, János. 1971. *Anti-equilibrium (On Economic Systems: Theory and the Tasks of Research)*. Amsterdam: North-Holland Publishing.

Kornai, János. 1972. *Rush Versus Harmonic Growth: Meditation on the Theory and on the Policies of Economic Growth*. Amsterdam and London: North-Holland Publishing.

Kornai, János. 1980. *Economics of Shortage*. Amsterdam: North Holland Publishers.

Kornai, János. 1992. *The Socialist System*. Princeton: Princeton University Press.

Kornai, János. 2016. So What Is Capital in the Twenty-First Century? Some Notes on Piketty's Book. *Capitalism & Society* 11 (1).

Krueger, Anne O. 1974. The Political Economy of Rent Seeking Society. *American Economic Review* 64 (3): 291–303.

Krugman, Paul. 2014. Why We're in a New Gilded Age. *The New York Review of Books*, May 4.

Kuznets, Simon. 1955. Economic Growth and Income Inequality. *American Economic Review* 1: 1–28.

Lenin, V.I. [1916] 2010. *Imperialism, the Highest Stage of Capitalism*. London: Penguin.

Levitt, Theodore. 1983. Globalization of Markets. *Harvard Business Review*, May–June.

Lewis, William. 2004. *The Power of Productivity: Wealth, Poverty, and the Threat to Global Stability*. Chicago: The University of Chicago Press.

Lindsey, Brink, and Steven M. Teles. 2017. *The Captured Economy (How the Powerful Enrich Themselves, Slow Down Growth and Increase Inequality)*. New York: Oxford University Press.

Lipset, Seymour Martin. [1960] 1981. *Political Man*. Baltimore: Johns Hopkins University Press.

Locke, John. [1698] 1988. *Two Treatise of Government*. Cambridge: Cambridge University Press.

Macrae, Norman. 1983. Into Entrepreneurial Socialism. *The Economist*, March 19, pp. 23–29.

Magyar, Bálint. 2016. *Post-communist Mafia State*. Budapest: Central European University Press.

Manza, Jeff, and Ned Crowley. 2017. Working Class Hero? Interrogation the Social Base of the Rise of Donald Trump. *The Forum* 15 (1): 3–28.

Marshall, Alfred. 1920. *Principles of Economics*, 8th ed. London: Macmillan.

Marx, Karl. [1867] 1954. *Capital*, Vol. I. Moscow: Progress Publishers.

Marx, Karl. [1885] 1956. *Capital*, Vol. II. Moscow: Progress Publishers.

Marx, Karl. [1894] 1959. *Capital*, Vol. III. Moscow: Progress Publishers.

Marx, Karl, and Friedrich Engels. 1848. *Manifesto of the Communist Party*. https://www.marxists.org/archive/marx/works/download/pdf/Manifesto.pdf.

McKinsey Global Institute (MGI). 2016. *People on the Move: Global Migration's Impact and Opportunity*. MGI.

Mihályi, Péter. 2001. The Evolution of Hungary's Approach to FDI in Post-communist Privatization. *Transnational Corporations* 3: 61–74.

Mihályi, Péter, and Iván Szelényi. 2016a. Two Different Sources of Inequalities: Profits and Rents in Advanced Market Economies. Hungarian Academy of Sciences Discussion Papers, MT-DP—2016/30, August, Institute of Economics, Centre for Economic and Regional Studies.

Mihályi, Péter, and Iván Szelényi. 2016b. Wealth and Capital: A Critique of Piketty's Conceptualisation of Return on Capital. *Cambridge Journal of Economics* (12). December. https://doi.org/10.1093/cje/bew054.

Mihályi, Péter, and Iván Szelényi. 2016c. Az egyenlőtlenségek valódi természetéről [On the True Nature of Inequalities]. *Mozgó Világ*, 11. sz. 3–12 (in Hungarian).

Mihályi, Péter, and Iván Szelényi. 2016d. Járadékvadászat Nyugaton és Keleten [Rent-Seeking in East and West], *168 óra*, No. 31. August 4, pp. 40–41 (in Hungarian).

Mihályi, Péter, and Iván Szelényi. 2017. The Role of Rents in the Transition from Socialist Redistributive Economies to Market Capitalism. *Comparative Sociology* 16: 13–38.

Milanovic, Branko. 2016. *Global Inequality: A New Approach for the Age of Globalization*. Cambridge: Harvard University Press.

Mitnik, Pablo, David Grusky, et al. 2015. New Estimates on Intergenerational Mobility Using Administrative Data. IRS Working Paper, Washington, DC. www.irs.gov/pub/irs-soi/15rpintergenmobility.pdf.

Moseley, F. 2014. Piketty and Marginal Productivity Theory: A Superficial Application of a Very Bad Theory. Manuscript. https://www.aeaweb.org/conference/2015/retrieve.php?pdfid=942. Date last accessed 5 December 2016.

North, Douglass C., John Joseph Wallis, and Barry R. Weingast. 2006. A Conceptual Framework for Interpreting Recorded Human History. NBER Working Paper 12795.

North, Duglas, John Joseph Wallis. Steven B. Webbs, and Berry Weinsgast. [2009] 2012. *Violence and Social Order*. Cambridge: Cambridge University Press.

OECD. 2015. *In It Together, Why Less Inequality Benefits All*. Paris: OECD Publishing. https://doi.org/10.1787/9789264235120-en.

Oliver, Mancur. 1995. *Black Wealth/White Wealth: A New Perspective on Racial Inequality*. New York: Routledge.

Olson, Mancur. 1982. *The Rise and Decline of Nations*. New Haven, CT: Yale University Press.

Ostry, J., A. Berg, and C.G. Tsangarides. 2014. *Redistribution, Inequality, and Growth*. IMF Staff Discussion Note.

Pareto, Vilfredo. [1916] 1935. *The Mind and Society* (Trattato Di Sociologia General). New York: Harcourt, Brace.

Pearson, Helen. 2016. *The Life Project: The Extraordinary Story of Our Ordinary Lives*. New York: Soft Skull Press.

Petersen, Trond. 2004. Aage Røttger Sørebsen's Contributions to Quantitative Sociology from Studying Processes to Studying Structure. *Research in Social Stratification* 21: 27–44.

Petersen, Trond. 2009. Opportunities. In *The Oxford Handbook of Analytical Sociology*, ed. Om Peter Hedström and Peter Bearman, Chapter 6, 115–139. Oxford: Oxford University Press.

Piketty, Thomas. 2014. *Capital in the Twenty-First Century*. Cambridge: Harvard University Press.

Piketty, Thomas, Emmanuel Saez, and Gabriel Zucman. 2016. Economic Growth in the United States: A Tale of Two Countries. Washington Center for Equitable Growth, December. http://equitablegrowth.org/research-analysis/economic-growth-in-the-united-states-a-tale-of-two-countries/.

Piketty, Thomas. 2018. Brahmin Left vs. Merchant Right: Rising Inequality in the Changing Structure of Political Conflict. WID Working Papers Series No. 7.

Pirvu, D. 2015. Corruption: Profile of Political Companies in Romania. *Acta Oeconomica* 65 (1, Special issue): 65–82.

Polanyi, Karl. 1944. *The Great Transformation.* New York: Farrar and Rinehart.

Polanyi, Karl. 1957. The Economy as an Instituted Process. In *Trade and Market in Early Empires*, ed. Karl Polanyi, Conrad Arendberg, and Harry W. Pearson, 243–270. New York: Free Press.

Polanyi, Karl. 1966. *Dahomey and the Slave Trade.* Seattle: University of Washington Press.

Posner, Eric A., and E. Glen Weyl. 2018. *Radical Markets Uprooting Capitalism and Democracy for a Just Society.* Princeton: Princeton University Press.

Posner, Richard A. 1975. The Social Costs on Monopoly and Regulation. *The Journal of Political Economy* 4: 807–828.

Posner, Richard A. 2009. *A Failure of Capitalism.* Cambridge: Harvard University Press.

Putnam, Robert D. 2015. *Our Kids: The American Dream in Crisis.* New York: Simon & Schuster.

Reeves, Martin, Mike Deimler, George Stalk, and Filippo L. Scognamiglio Pasini. 2012. BCG Classics Revisited, the Rule of Three and Four. www.bcgperspectives.com/content/articles/business_unit_strategy_the_rule_of_three_and_four_bcg_classics_revisited/.

Reeves, E. Richard. 2017. *Dream Hoarders: How the American Upper Middle Class Is Leaving Everyone Else in the Dust, Why That Is a Problem, and What to Do About It.* Washington, DC: Brookings Institution Press.

Ricardo, David. [1817] 2004. *Principles of Political Economy and Taxation.* Mineola, NY: Dover Publications.

Riviera, Lauren A. 2015. *Pedigree: How Elite Students Get Elite Jobs.* Princeton: Princeton University Press.

Rodrik, Dani. 2013. The Past, Present, and Future of Economic Convergence. http://www.sss.ias.edu/files/pdfs/Rodrik/Presentations/Past-Present-and-Future-Economic-Convergence-(October2013).pdf.

Roemer, John. 1982. *A General Theory of Exploitation and Class.* Cambridge, MA: Harvard University Press.

Roth, Guenther. 1978. *Economy and Society*, ed. Max Weber, Footnote #67 to Volume 1, Chapter II, p. 211. Berkeley: University of California Press.

Schwarz, Christine R., and Robert Mare. 2005. Trend in Educational Assortative Marriage from 1940 to 2003. *Demography* 42: 621–646.

Sen, Amartya. 1990. More Than 100 Million Women Are Missing. *The New York Review of Books* 37 (20) 61–66.

Sen, Amartya. 1992. Missing Women. *British Medical Journal* 304: 586–587.

Smith, Adam. [1776] 1976. *The Wealth of Nations.* Chicago: The University of Chicago Press.

Smyth, Don. 1984. Achievements, New Directions from 1994 ILO Conference. *Monthly Labor Review*, September.

Solow, Robert. 2014. Thomas Piketty Is Right. *New Republic*, April 22.

Solow, Robert. 2015. The Future of Work, Why Wages Aren't Keeping Up? *Pacific Standard*, August 11.

Sorensen, Aage B. 1996. The Structural Basis of Inequality. *American Journal of Sociology* 101 (5): 1333–1365.

Sorensen, Aage B. 2000. Toward a Sounder Basis for Class Analysis. *American Journal of Sociology* 6: 1523–1558.

Standing, Guy. 2017. *Basic Income*. New Haven: Yale University Press.

Staniszkis, J. 1991. Political Capitalism in Poland. *East European Politics and Societies* 1: 127–141.

Stanley, T., and W. Danko. 1998. *The Millionaire Next Door, the Surprising Secrets of America's Wealthy*. New York: Simon & Schuster.

Stark, David. 1996. Recombinant Property in East European Capitalism. *American Journal of Sociology* 101 (4): 492–504.

Stigler, George. 1971. The Theory of Economic Regulation. *The Bell Journal of Economics and Management Science* 2 (Spring) (1): 3–21.

Stiglitz, Joseph. 1977. The Theory of Local Public Goods. In *The Economics of Public Goods*, ed. M.S. Feldstein and R.P. Inman, 274–333. London: Macmillan.

Stiglitz, Joseph. 1992. *Economics*. New York and London: W.W. Norton.

Stiglitz, Joseph. 2002. *Globalization and Its Discontents*. New York: W.W. Norton.

Stiglitz, Joseph. 2006. *Making Globalization Work*. New York: W.W. Norton.

Stiglitz, Joseph. 2012. *The Price of Inequality*. New York: W.W. Norton.

Stiglitz, Joseph. 2015a. New Theoretical Perspectives on the Distribution of Income and Wealth Among Individuals, Parts I–IV. NBER Working Paper Series, 21189, 21190, 21191, 21192.

Stiglitz, Joseph. 2015b. The Origins of Inequality, and Policies to Contain It. *National Tax Journal* 68 (2): 425–448.

Szalai, Erzsébet. 1989. The New Elite. *Across Frontiers* 5: 25–31.

Szelényi, Iván. 2010. The New Grand Bourgeoisie Under Post-communism: Central Europe, Russia and China Compared. Working Paper No. 2010/63, United Nations University, World Institute for Development Economic Research, Helsinki.

Szelényi, Iván. 2015. Thomas Piketty: A Tőke a 21. században. *Budapesti Könyvszemle* (1–2): 80–84 (in Hungarian).

Szelényi, Iván (in collaboration with Riaz Hassan and Vladislav Maksimov). 2018. *Building Nations with Non-nationals: The Exclusionary Immigration Regimes of the Gulf Monarchies with a Case study of Pakistani Return Migrants from and Prospective Migrants to the United Arab Emirates*. Budapest: Corvina.

Townsley, Eleanor. 2009. *The Sociology of Intellectual Life: The Career of the Mind in and Around Academy*. London: Sage.

Tóth, István György. 2014. Revisiting Grand Narratives of Growing Income Inequalities: Lessons from 30 Country Studies. In *Changing Inequalities and Societal Impacts in Rich Countries: Thirty Countries' Experiences*, ed. B. Nolan, W. Salverda, D. Checchi, I. Marx, A. Mcknight, I. Gy. Tóth, and H. G. van de Werfhorst, 11–47. Oxford: Oxford University Press.

Tullock, G. 1967. The Welfare Costs of Tariffs, Monopolies and Theft. *Western Economic Journal* 5 (3): 224–232.

Tullock, Gordon. 1980. Rent-Seeking as a Negative-Sum Game. In *Toward a Theory of Rent-Seeking Society*, ed. James Buchanan, Robert D. Tollison, and Gordon Tullock, 16–38. College Station: Texas A&M University Press.

Vaughan-Whitehead, Daniel (ed.). 2016. Europe's Disappearing Middle Class? Evidence from the World of Work. Cheltenham, UK and Northampton, MA, USA: Edward Elgar Publishing and Geneva: International Labour Office.

Wallerstein, Immanuel. 1974. *The Modern World System*. New York: Academic Press.

Weber, Max [1908] 1986. *The Agrarian History and Ancient Civilization*. [Agrarverhältnisse im Altertum (3. Fassung)]. London: Verso (German Edition MWG Band 6. pp. 320–751. Tübingen: J.C.B Mohr, 2006).

Weber, Max. [1921] 1978. *Economy and Society*. Berkeley, CA: University of California Press.

Weber, Max. [1921] 2013. *Wirtschaft und Gesellschaft. Soziologie: Max Weber Gesamtausgabe*, Band 23. Tübingen: J.C.B. Mohr.

Weeden, Kim A., and David Grusky. 2014. Inequality and Market Failure. *American Behavioral Scientist* 58 (3): 473–491.

Whyte, Martin K. 2010. *Myth of the Social Volcano*. Stanford: Stanford University Press.

World Bank. 2013. *End Extreme Poverty and Promote Shared Prosperity*. Washington, DC: The World Bank. http://www.worldbank.org/content/dam/Worldbank/document/WB-goals2013.pdf.

Wright, Erik Olin. 1985. *Classes*. London: New Left Books.

Zakaria, Fareed. 1997. The Rise of Illiberal Democracy. *Foreign Affairs* 76 (6): 22–43.

Author Index

P. Mihályi and I. Szelényi,
Rent-Seekers, Profits, Wages and Inequality,
https://doi.org/10.1007/978-3-030-03846-5

Subject Index

P. Mihályi and I. Szelényi,
Rent-Seekers, Profits, Wages and Inequality,
https://doi.org/10.1007/978-3-030-03846-5

The manufacturer's authorised representative in the EU is Springer Nature Customer Service Centre GmbH, Europaplatz 3, 69115 Heidelberg, Germany. If you have any concerns regarding our products, please contact ProductSafety@springernature.com

Printed and bound by CPI Group (UK) Ltd, Croydon, CR0 4YY

30/09/2026

02225466-0013